COMPARATIVE STUDY OF SELECTED FEMALE WRITERS

AS SEEN IN THE GLOBAL PERSPECTIVE

Jane O. O. Landey

ISBN-13: 978-1500686987

Printed in U.S.A.

ACKNOWLEDGEMENTS

I am indeed happy to publish this literary work because it is a topic of my doctoral thesis: Comparative Study of Female Writers as Seen in the Global Perspective. Reading through, I feel it would be useful to those who want to know about outstanding female writers who had written exceptional stories read worldwide. My appreciation goes to the Almighty God who enables me to start writing after five years of doctoral program and teaching with University of Abomey, Calavi, Republic of Benin. There is a lot to say about my Head of Department, Dr. Taofik Koumapai, who guided my activities and was always there to give one advice or the other. May Almighty God, prosper him and his family every moment. I thank Dr. Afanouh for using the Black Maiden as one of the first year recommended text and all the students that reviewed it.

Professor Akachi Adimora Ezeigbo, being the external supervisor of this thesis, thanks and recognition are accorded for all the books and articles she gave me to be able to write effectively on this topic.

The short poem is dedicated to her to show my appreciation.

> More grease to your elbow
>
> A woman of substance and virtue
>
> One who, both gender adore to be
>
> To you, honorable Akachi Adimora Ezeigbo.

Moreover, I extend thanks to my father, Rev. Olu Emmanuel, who assisted financially and materially. God will lengthen your days.

INTRODUCTION

The topic is basically on the writings of different viable authors who proved their worth in different engagements accorded to themselves. People in different places are familiar with writings of personalities in dire transformation of the society. There is no doubt therefore, that due to them, there had been changes or reformations in these vicinities. There had been practically, series of instances where writings had not only influenced the readers but had also transformed their lives too. Recorded events in places, for instance, where there were misinterpretations sprouting from the authorities of the governing bodies that criticized, equally felt not favored and honored. The reaction for such abusive attitude was imprisonment for such piece of writing.

There is always the urge to write extensively on oppression and injustice when the compassion is evident. Nevertheless, many ardent writers saw existence in different perspectives which were based on cultural norms and attributes. Many literary works were not favorably written and circumstances surrounding their writing periods were not equally pleasant. Many writers went through torment and dejection from the people they tried to defend. There were series of styles used by each viable author to convey messages to their readers.

This is a general knowledge on writers of old and new who are men and women. Each has defensive motive and desire portrayed in capturing the minds of their readers, through artistic and visual means. In other words, readers are able to transform and transmit the message as regarded by the writer and equally hold on to it.

Most literary works were emotionally written, the waves flow to the readers and listeners. In this case, there is a great change or influence. Societies are transformed by such pieces of ideas in writing forms.

Messages transmitted are either negative or positive which could hinder the progress or influence national orientation. Writers could be termed the messiahs of the people who lay their lives for the masses.

The topic of this thesis is, Comparative Study of Selected Female Writers as Seen in the Global Perspective. The following female writers will be our focus. Jane Austen's novels such as Pride and Prejudice, Emma, Persuasion, Mansfield Park, Sense and Sensibility will be dealt with in this literary work. Jane Austen novels are notable for ethics and moral attributes. In the prime of her time, women, especially men were held in high esteem by their characters. Many also feel her works have some prestigious style of her time. Characters in Pride and Prejudice were elegantly presented but morally enriched. The qualities she posed were good for the time but ones that yield continuity in whomever come across, could have been better. Moreover, the time of her writing the readers could see the interest she took in her characters. All the characters seen in her novels were traced to her and her family in which she portrayed each character distinctively. The second writer, is Charlotte Bronte, who wrote arbitrarily, novels that depicted the test of time. She presented conveniently, emotional touch on her characters. Here are some of some of her novels, Jane Eyre, The Professor, Villette and Miss Percy. Reading through her novels, one could see there was airy moment of compassion, love and hatred.

In her own case, she revealed individual comportment and nature as seen in Jane Eyre, who is the prominent character. Charlotte Bronte could not be seen as a writer of her time but one who led women to start writing. Her influence on other females was evidently established and made it to the end even at her dying age. During the reign of Victoria, in the eighteen century, women were not educated or to have public interaction, but the ardent Queen Victoria really encouraged women to take their stand. Charlotte Bronte went ahead to make women publicly reveal their opinions. Thus, began the uniformity with men. The two writers were British who lived in different moments, they wrote for individual growth and personality. Their writings portrayed women who were faced with the difficulty of the time they found themselves and public influence. Consequently, this influence on women paved way for humanity. Alberta Wilson Constant wrote for the young people of her time in her area in United States of America. A writer of the twentieth century wrote popular and highly acclaimed novels, all of which have richly authentic turn-of-the century. The novels Does Anyone Care About Lou Emma Miller, The Motoring Millers and Those Miler Girls would be the focus for this thesis. All her writings have American background, whereby they carried the need for American growth.

Lou Emma Miller was a character aggravated to another character. Ironically, though she wrote for the young, not withstanding her focus was on the debate of establishing the women too.

Joyce Carol Oates as one of the world's most eminent authors, suggest a feminist literary version of the mythic pursuit and achievement of American dream. Her three Gothic novel used in this thesis, are awareness of absence of morality, justice and purity. Bellefleur indicates excessive mismanagement and non charlatan attitude. A Bloodsmoor Romance is evidently, the waywardness of youths and a society losing its validity. In the world of A Bloodsmoor Romance, time machines run rampant, transcendegitalism gives way to the spirit world and decorum and etiquette fall to the exigencies of passions.

Mysteries of Winterthurn exposes the reader to one man's determination to hunt for the murderers of innocent people. Going back to his root, Winterthurn, where he was born, enables him to know more about his origin. Xavier represents the law or justice while Perdita represents the new land, America, which suffers in the hand of its exploiters. Joyce Carol Oates has been able to capture the vision, "Post America."

The means justify the end, coming to Africa, which is the home of festivity and cultural display. A continent of tradition and culture are interwoven despite the era of civilization. Africa, a region full of wild life, reflecting in the appearance and attitude of the inhabitants. Nevertheless, colonization, has paved way for modernism, thus, enabling women to write about their cultures and effects through the education they acquired. Akachi Adimora Ezeigbo and Jane Olamide Olubunmi are the two female writers that will be the focus in this thesis. They have both written extensively on women though in different dimensions.

Akachi Adimora Ezeigbo's trilogy is eloquently and distinctively written. Somehow her characters are not isolated but attributes of marriage and family extension are evident where men and women play vital roles.

There are female heroes as seen in the Last of the Strong Ones. The trilogy has given the readers insight into her different outstanding literary works. House of Symbols and Children of the Eagles are very remarkable.

Jane Olamide Olubunmi is a prolific writer of the twentieth and twenty first centuries. Her works were not published until 2004, though she started writing in 1991. She is a literary writer who artistically portrayed her characters vividly in the limelight of tradition and culture of her tribe. She has reinforced the beauty of her culture in the eye of the beholder. Her first three literary works converged to a trilogy of pre-colonial to the post-colonial eras. The literary works she has written would be the focus in this thesis, Black Maiden, Here at Last and The Eagle. Here, her revelations of stereotype and round characters with strong effects of romance and wars. The structure and style make the stories interesting.

SUMMARY OF EACH FEMALE'S TEXT

JANE AUSTEN: Pride And Prejudice

      Emma

      Persuasion

      Man's Field Park

      Sense And Sensibility

Opening an Austen novel is entering a tight little world where you may have money but you must have manners, where the Napoleonic wars may be going on somewhere outside, but the rhythm of an established social life is undisturbed. Not all her people are intelligent; indeed, there are some of her bores, Mr. Collins, the perfect specimen of bore, in Pride And Prejudice, or Miss Bates in Emma, whose long distance record in sentences runs two full pages, unimpeded by more than dashes and an occasional comma. Yet my copy of Emma falls open of itself at this speech and really account of the party at which it was also uttered. Mrs. Norris in Man's Field Park is a tyrannical old cat, but also need not meet her in person; I do love to hear her expose herself in conversation.

Those people use an English so charming you long fervently to bring back to their true meaning some of the ardent words-they use to make "eloquent" again a word meaning grace and refinement, and not the ever wanted adjective we

use today as "good" or "first" _ rate"; to make "candor" once more an honest word for justice and fairness rather than tactless truth-telling.

All Jane Austen's heroines are better than perfect; they are deliciously human. When you begin with Elizabeth Bennet of Pride And Prejudice you start at the top. I say this with a slight feeling of disloyalty to my friend Emma in the novel named for her, to dear Anne Eliot in Persuasion, and to Elinor and Marriane of Sense And Sensibility. But after all, there is only Elizabeth Bennet.

Pride and Prejudice relates all that happen to each character, the quality of the novel is very glaring. There are other good novels such as Emma, Man's Field Park,

Persuasion and Sense And Sensibility. There is always the reflection of Jane Austin in each novel. This realization, gives us the nature of the writer with ease. One should not forget that, speech and thoughts within her are equally portrayed.

I like to think that Jane Austen herself was al unconsciously drawing something very like her portrait in Lizzy, and of one thing we can be sure-that in Jane, the eldest Miss Bennet, the essential traits of character are those of Miss Austen's sister Cassandra. Lizzy's loving admiration of Austen's qualities is the very same the author shows, in her letters, to her own dear, devoted sister. I have never tried to identify

Darcy, he is to me the hero of the most amazing proposal of marriage in the nineteenth century fiction.

Jane Austen was a true artist at creating proposal scenes, and she must have had several on her own account, but none of them was ever accepted. She remains to us "dear, delighted Jane" with no other name than the one she started with.

Let us look at each novel critically. Pride and Prejudice denotes the life of a young girl, named Lizzy as been opted out from among Mr. and Mrs. Bennet's daughters.

Mr. Bennet seems to want one of his daughters married to the new occupant of Netherland Park. He is a rich man, young with a large fortune from the North of England. Bingley as his name implies, seems to have a different idea, such is revealed in the novel.

"Bingley had never met with pleasanter people or prettier girls in his life; everyone had been most kind and attentive to him, there had been no formality, no stiffness, he had soon felt acquainted with all the room; and as to Miss Bennet, he could not conceive an angel more beautiful. Three groups of people are interested in the new occupant of Netherfield Park, Mr. Bingley. They are: The parents of most beautiful girls in the neighborhood, such as Mr. and

Mrs. Bennet, Mr. and Mrs. Lucas who have several children, and the ladies of Longbourn.

Secondly, the young girls of Longbourn, the Bennets, the Lucases, Miss King and the Boulanger. Thirdly, the residence of Hertfordshire, These are the excerpts which show the pronunciation of each group.

"That the Miss Lucas and the Miss Bennets should meet to talk over a ball was absolutely necessary; and the morning after the assembly brought the former to Longbourn to hear and communicate. "You began the evening well, Charlotte," said Mrs. Bennet with civil self-command to Miss Lucas.

"You were Mr. Bingley first choice." "Yes; but he seemed to like his second better.

Mr. Bingley admiration of Jane is summed up in his words and actions. When Jane slightly recovered, he is all attention. Thus the excerpt:

> "His intentions to herself most pleasing and
>
> they prevented her feeling herself so mush
>
> an intruder as she believed she was considered
>
> by others. She had a little notice
>
> from any but him."

Mr. Bingley engages the lady servants to pay attention to Jane and Elizabeth. This shows his affection for Jane and the Bennets family. Mrs. Bennet being summoned by Elizabeth, shows the love of the girls for Netherfield Park. Mrs. Bennet on the other hand, is so anxious for the Bloom of love to spark between Mr. Bingley and Jane. Thus, the obvious statement:

> "Bingley met them with hopes that Mrs. Bennet
>
> had not found Miss Bennet worse than she expected."
>
> She replied, "indeed I have, Sir," was her answer.
>
> Mrs. Jones says we must not think of moving her.
>
> We must trespass a little longer on your kindness."
>
> Mr. Bingley is really pleased to confirm it.
>
> "Removed!" Cried Bingley. "It must
>
> Not be thought of............"

Everybody's admiration for Netherfield Park is evident. Mrs. Bennet is told about Sir Williams and daughter, Charlotte visiting the Bingley. She feels Mr. Bingley acquaints himself with everybody She says this about him:

> "He has always something to say to everybody."

Though Mr. Bingley sees Charlotte pleasant, he realizes Jane's beauty. Mrs.Bennet bluntly lashes out the difference. "But everybody is to judge for themselves

and the Lucases are very good sort of girls,

I assure you. It is a pit they are not handsome!

Bingley replies : She seems a very pleasant woman,"

Mrs. Bennet continues: "Oh! Dear, yes; but you must own she is very plain.

Lady Lucas herself has often said so, and envied my

Jane's beauty. I do not like to boast of my own child

but to be sure? Jane- one does not often see

anybody better looking." "However, little known the

feeling of views of such a man may be entering a

neighborhood, this truth is so well fixed in the minds

of the surrounding families that he is considered as the

rightful property of someone or other of their daughters.

Mr. Bingley has two sisters who arrive with him in Netherfield Park. Accompanied are his eldest sister's husband, Mr. Hurst and his friend, Mr. Darcy. Mr. Darcy is seen more adorable than Mr. Bingley thus the following remark:

> "The gentlemen pronounced him to be a fine figure of a man, the ladies declared he was much handsome than Mr. Bingley....."

The invitation from Mr. Bingley inviting Jane to dinner ignited a relationship between Mr. Bingley and Jane. Elizabeth searched for her sister who has not returned from such invitation leads to Mr. Darcy becoming more acquainted with her. Jane's sickness and remaining in bed, in the Bingley family is a delight to the Bennet's family. Mr. Bingley is delighted to have her under roof and when Elizabeth comes to know what has become of her sister, Jane, feels so disappointed and would not hear of her being taken away at such precarious moment. Elizabeth relaxes to enjoy her stay in the Bingleys home. Few words and interaction pass between Mr. Darcy and Elizabeth.

> Now: "Then, observed Elizabeth, you must comprehend a great deal in your idea of an accomplished woman."

Mr. Darcy replies: "Yes, I do comprehend a great deal in it.

"Oh! Certainly," cried his faithful assistance.

"No one can be really esteemed accomplished who does not greatly surpass what is usually met with. A woman must have a thorough knowledge of music, Singing, drawing, dancing, and the modern language, to deserve the word; and besides all this, she must possess a certain something in her air and manner of walking, the tone of her voice, her dress and expressions, or the word will be half half-deserved."

"All this she must possess," added Darcy.

EMMA:

It was published at the end of 1815. It contains three volumes. There is the major character Emma and some others such as,Mr. Knightley, Mr. Elton, Mr. Woodhouse, Mrs. Weston, Robert Marton, Harriet Smith and Miss Smith, Emma's favorite.

Harriet seems awful fond of Mr. Knightley but Emma is not.

She takes to Mr. Elton: "What an excellent likeness of Mr. Elton."

Mr. Knightley dominating and dictating the future of Emma irritates her even though she cannot stop the old man from it.

Life in Randalls is full of festivities such as balls and marriages. There are new arrivals that seem fitted into the activities. Jane Fairfax coming to live in Randalls Mr. Knightley approving the proposal of Mr. Elton. The wedding is like any other that has been celebrated in Randalls. The latest couples engaged of the three to be married are Harriet Smith and Robert Marton. The news is pretty unacceptable to Emma who feels they are incompatible.

> "Well, now tell me everything, make this
>
> Intelligible to me. How, where, when?
>
> Let me know all.
>
> …….How was it been possible.

Emma is not regarded with high esteem as Harriet by most young men and though she fancies her cousin Frank Churchill. She thinks a lot about him. An observation from some one:

> "Happy is the man who changes
>
> Emma for Harriet."

She trusts Miss Smith more than the other characters in the novel. It is not possible for her to confide in Miss Smith about her love for Frank. Now she has been warned not to go to such extent, it is not possible for the two of them to think about marriage. The three young ladies are presented differently- Emma is very arrogant, Jane Fairfax is very snobbish, Isabella is non-charlatan and Harriet Smith seems very charming. She is the character many men admire. The reason Robert asks her to marry him. These other characters have played important roles in the novel, Miss Hawkins, Mr. Martin, the Campbell and the Churchills who cannot wait to witness the wedding in Randalls.

Jane Austen concludes the story by this expression:

"Who can be in doubt of what followed?

When any two young people take it into

 their heads to marry.

PERSUASION

This novel is written by Jane Austen between August 1815 and 1816. It was published by her brother Henry Austen after her death. He had long been champion of his sister's work. The novel contains two volumes.

The notable towns where the events take place are.
Lynne and Kelynch.

The characters in the novel are, Annee, the focus, Elizabeth
and Mar, sisters of Annee, Mr. Elliot, their father, Lady
Russell, Mrs. Clay, Mrs. Smith, a widow, Hrville, Benwick, and
Charles Hauter. Each has a role to play either as a governess,
friend or suitor to the members of the Elliots.

Mr. Elliot has a financial problem and is compelled to let out
the house to Frederick Worthorth who used to be a close
friend of Annee. Frederik taking over the house and thus
Annee thinking they can make up the past as suggested by
him is to no avail. The arrival of the Dalrymples creates
companions for the Elliots. They receive the Elliots
cheerfully which is a sign of good company. Looking back at
the Elliots' life, when Mr. Elliot has financial problem, the
family go off to Bath and Annee goes off to Uppercross,
Frederick arrives and meets Annee again. The question
springs up, who will Frederick pick, Henrietta or Louisa?

Eventually, Harville and Annee engage and "they discuss
constancy of love." "You pierce my soul." Annee marries
Captain Wentworth, she glories in being a sailor's wife.

Elizabeth and Mary, after such persuasion get
themselves engaged to Charles Hauter and Captain
Benwick respectively.

Jane Austen is traditionally, associated with the Victorian period but actually lived prior to it. Most Jane Austen's books were published during the Regency or Georgian Period but since she influenced the thinking of so many Victorians, some believe that her work should be taught with that of later novels. Austen was more particularly concerned with domestic life, especially where it concerned the situation of women.

MANSFIELD PARK:

The story in this novel is growing up of a young girl, named Fanny in a family not like her. Miss Bertrams seems to find Fanny, insipid and priggish. Inability to acknowledge certain facts of understanding makes her a stupid person before them.

Leaving her family behind to be driven down to Mansfield Park is not to her delight. The idea being exchanged between her mother and Mrs. Bertram and Mrs. Norris is without her knowledge until she finds herself leaving Portsmouth to Mansfield. Fanny's mother who has just given birth to the ninth child realizes the assistance her two sisters will be offering if they add her second child to their family.

Fanny's father, recently jobless and a drunkard has made life unbearable for her. William her first child and very dear to her, is more of a son. She calls him" My little darling."

The arrival of Fanny in Mansfield is at first disregarded, Sir Thomas feels Fanny will influence the two girls, Julia and Maria.

"Afraid of everybody, ashamed of herself,

And longing for the home she had left."

Edmund relieves Fanny of the longing for her home by assisting her in writing to her beloved brother William. Edmund comes closer and Fanny gets fonder of him.

"Loving, guiding, protecting her…….."

Fanny is not like the lively and witty Elizabeth Bennet of Pride and Prejudice. The complexity of the themes has brought about the admiration of the readers. The heroine, a young woman is unlike any of her novels. Her brother Williams pays a visit after many years of separation. His departure is very painful. Fanny visits her family in Portsmouth, she has to return because there is a new life she lives now. The end of the story is remarkable after much ado. Julia elopes with Yates to Scotland while Mary remains at home. Edmund breaks off with Miss Crawford. He suffers disappointment and regret. Sir Thomas and Mrs. Bertram have very much taken to Fanny and they want her always in Mansfield Park. Back home, everything is going well for her parents Mr. and Mrs. Price, her brother William has become a sailor and most importantly, she regains her love for Edmund.

More characters in the novel are, Mrs. Rushworth, Mrs. Crawford, Henry, Mr. and Mrs. Norris, Tom, the second son of the Bertrams. All of them have contributed to the events in the story.

SENSE AND SENSIBILITY

The novel was written in the late 18th century. Its primary concern is the lives of two sisters, Elinor and Marianne Dashwood. Elinnor has too much sense and Marianne is more sympathetic. Agony of grief overpowered them at first says the narrator of Miss Dashwood and Marianne's response to the death of Mr. Dashwood "was voluntary renewed, was sought for, was created again and again.

Marriage in the story:

Charlotte and Palmer

Fanny and John Dashwood.

Lucy Steeke and Robert Ferrars

Elinor and Edward

Marianne and Brandon

Losing their father is a great blow and the sisters and their mother resort to continue living with what life can bring. Elinor, regarding herself sensible encourages Edward, s love. She sees a refuge in what Marianne terms as:

" Money can only give happiness when there is

Nothing else to give it."

Elinor sees love differently,

"Wealth has much to do with unhappiness."

The novel relates balancing emotions and thoughts. Elinor does things irrationally, although her actions make sense. Marianne gives thought to her actions before carrying them out. Marianne wants to continue to live with her mother but the intervention of Bradon makes her to think about Marriage as the ultimate goal. Love means much to her unlike Elinor who feels wealth is the foundation of love.

Jane Austin depicts marriage as the ultimate goal and happy ending for Elinor and Marianne.

CHARLOTTE BRONTE

Jane Eyre

The Professor

Villette

Miss Percy

The Gothic romance of Jane Eyre through the 1847 novel was not intended as a genre piece. The unconventionality of the heroine and the tormented unscrupulousness of Rochester(whose bigamy may be immoral but is also an attempt to restore love and sanity to life) shocked many of its readers. The opening of the book, deals with the oppressed existence of the orphaned Jane in a household of cruel relatives. It is seen how she is roughed up by the vicious little beasts who are her cousins and thrust into a closet where she turns round and round in helpless bewilderment. It is a pathetic enough image but it is also exactly the sort of thing we expect in any life about orphans. Little Jane is indeed baited by her beastly male cousin, and what does the helpless little girl-child do? Why, she pounces upon the much larger boy and proceeds to beat the daylights out of him. This is how Jane Eyre's independence of mind and spirit first manifests itself- as sheer physical wrath, as scratching and biting, as animal revolt.

Later, Jane learned of Rochester's mad wife and her dream of marital happiness shatters. She leaves her lover's estate. Jane leaves on foot and with nothing but the clothes on her back, abandoning herself to the inclemency of weather and the doubtful civility of anyone she encounters on the road. Her departure is radical in its rejection of Rochester, of hope, of prosperity, and almost of life itself. When Jane revolts, she goes all the way. She is an extremist heroine of an extremist book.

You can see why she is homely in an interesting way, self-contained, somewhat elfin (Rochester to Jane: "Oh Jane, you strange, unearthly thing!"), and the line of her mouth is a fascinating scribble. But appearance can never take the place of performance in the case of a major dramatic role. Her performance is absolutely static. The tail end of the novel, reads:" Our happiness is compete"...... sounds as if she were announcing funeral arrangements. Nor is the monotony purely vocal. When Rochester looks at Jane in her bridal gown and exclaims on her new beauty, no sense of freshly discovered womanliness or nascent sexuality emanates from Jane Eyre is to be subdued, not squashed.

MISS PERCY

Miss Percy is a pupil at M. Turner's seminary at Kessington. She is a lonely and sad girl, whose morality is Madame

Turner's concern. Her father does not only show off with his wealth but display it. He cares less about the poor girl who is bereaved of her mother. Percy, the little is the central character whose attributes belong to others. Madame Turner cannot have wished for any other pupil but Percy, whose father pays her school fee regularly. Percy's father cannot for once avoid seeing his daughter who enables him to show off his wealth whenever he visits her. The whole story is all about the little girl whose future lies in the palm of many.

Charlotte Bronte described how the major character in her novel.

THE PROFESSOR

The Professor must be, she reveals in the introduction,

> "I said to myself that my hero should work his way
>
> through life as I had seen real living men work their
>
> theirs- that he should never get a shilling he had
>
> not earned, that no sudden turns should lift him
>
> in a moment to wealth and high station, that
>
> whatever small competency he might gain,
>
> should be won by the sweat of his brow."

Thus The Professor is born. The long relationship between Francis and professor, William takes its shape from the pupil-teacher relationship. William teaching Francis how to read, write and speak English is not a one day effort but the gradual systematic procedure turns out to be more serious than fun.

The sadness experienced by from a previous relationship is gradually wiped off by her marriage to William, her English teacher. Mr. Vandenhnten , conducts the marriage in a chapel, one January morning. They both enjoy the early period of their marriage. They have dinner out often though leaving home early in the morning for work to return home, cordial and cosy home is a priority.

Mr. and Mrs. Crimsworth live up to expectation of their marriage. William cannot destroy totally the pupil-teacher relationship, hence he demands why Francis keeps calling him monsieur.

"Why do you always call me monsieur?" Says William.

"I cannot pronounce your name, besides 'monsieur' belongs to you;

I like it best." This is Francis reply.

Francis, though happy in her marriage, she seems to conceal in her, the past.

"I seemed to possess two wives- The faculties of nature already disclosed when I married her, remained fresh and fair, but other faculties shut up strong, branched out broad, and quite altered the external character of the plant."

William refers to Francis, his wife as madame who manages his home in the evening and school in day time.

"My home was my heaven."

Moving to English initiated them fully into the English culture and status. In Belgium, where they have started a school that is popular, energize them to send forth someone to establish another school in England. Mr. and Mrs. Crimsworth become to be known as proprietor and proprietress of a model school. "Victor their son was born in the third year of their marriage. They gave him the Christian name of their friend "Mr. M.Vandenhn. Charlortte Bronte's husband, A. B. Nicholls published The Professor and Villette after her death. He wrote a comment that the two novels are not related.

VILLETTE

A young girl called Lucy, is the dominant character, who narrates her story. The female character in the novel, has similar actions to Francis in The Professor. Lucy, the first person narrator like Jane Eyre creeps through life in trials.

She sees life differently when she lives with Brettons. Coming finally to stay in Villette, when she meets Professeur, is a boost to her ego.

> "My school flourishes, my home is ready,
>
> I have made him a little library, filled with
>
> the books he left in my care. I have cultivated
>
> out of love for him. I thought I love him when
>
> he was away, I love him now in another degree,
>
> he is my own."

Lucy Snowe has encountered relationships with many characters in the novel. Observation from the beginning of the story reveals Lucy living with the Bretton. Mrs. Bretton is her godmother. A widow who has children that Lucy knows as playmates. Paulina is one of Mr. Bretton's children. She keeps calling out to her father, "Papa, my dear papa."

Miss Marchment is another character, Lucy comes across. She maintains her loyalty when Lucy's wage is sent to he, a long distance cousin who takes over the property pays off all the outstanding debts.

Madame Beck's school is an exception because she engages in teaching the pupils German language. Here, she is fascinated by many characters like, Madame Panache, a temporal History teacher, Mr. Paul, who detests women and Emmanuel, known as Professeur.

Any reader's attention will be captivated by the relationship between Lucy and Emmanuel. Emmanuel's love is vividly shown by his utterances.

> "Lucy, take my love.
>
> One day, share my life.
>
> Be my dearest, first on earth."

Lucy cannot resist the affection she has for Emmanuel.

> "...........I thought I loved him when he was
>
> away, I love him in another degree........."

ALBERTA WILSON CONSTANT

DOES ANYBODY CARE ABOUT LOU EMMA MILLER?

THOSE MILLER GIRLS

THE MOTORING MILLERS

The novels of Alberta Wilson Constant are quite remarkable because she tries to link the infants with the adults. Reading through most of her novels, she relates to the effect that one realizes children should be given total concern. She has written effectively on American background. Mostly, there is denotation on female characters either on children or women. Summarizing the novel, Does Anybody Care About Lou Emma Miller? She presents women in any form as capable and efficient if given the opportunity. This is one of her bestselling novels. Emma, a young girl of fifteen years old seems to capture the attention of the readers even if her junior sister is claiming the attention of the entire family. In totality, Does Anybody Care About Lou Emma Miller? A woman running for mayor of Gloriosa? Some people in town think Mrs. Biddle's campaign is an outrage……..but Lou Emma Miller thinks it's one of the best things to have happened in Kansas since woman's suffrage.

Now if her candidate would decide to take seriously Lou Emma's idea for a town library- a library filled with books to read, not study. The trouble is, nobody seems to be taking notice of Lou Emma at all lately. Her inner meditation reflects this:

Maddy's pretty. Prettier 'n me.

Prettiest of all when she's like this."

When she runs after Tommy, her classmate, she feels all things are not done rightly by her, thus the utterance: Why is everything that's fun always the wrong thing for me to do?"

Everybody seems to know about her closeness to Tommy. "Walk me home," Adelaide suggests.

"Unless you think Tommy's coming.

She replies to hide the truth.

"I'm waiting for my Maddy. She's practicing debate with Demons."

Emma has a family comprising of a father, stepmother, a sister and a brother both of which are junior to her. Her father taught in a university while her stepmother owned a store where she made hats for women. Everyone in the family paid more attention to Maddy, who they felt was intelligent. Maddy on the other hand was very quick in assimilating and understanding exercises imposed on her at school.

Mr. Meadow cannot not hide his feelings about Maddy. He says "Good student, Maddy. Great at History. She recites well." Emma does not see it that way; she feels recitation is not brilliancy.

Thus : "Inside she snapped, reciting six times in class is showing off."

Miss Baker's remark about Emma when Mr. Meadow ended his remark, "Lou Emma is one of my best students." "She loves poetry. I think she may become a poet some day." Lou Emma treasures Miss Baker's words. "They made little bells in her heart." Tony's admiration for her helps her keep abreast and boost her ego. Emma's father, Professor Miller feels quite proud of his second daughter, though he gets bored with her recitation even when the family gathers for meals.

".......... But I'm a little tired of Maddy's oratory. How are you standing it?"

Miss Kate who is in the second marriage to professor Miller feels women should participate in the constitution. "Maybe it's time that young women debated it. Maybe we can make some changes."

Professor Miller agreed with Miss Kate. Thus: "You k now I agree with you and I want women to get the vote nationally, but Lou Emma seemed to be responsible for caring for her junior sister, Maddy. The death of their mother had turned her into a little mistress to their father until Miss Kate got married to their father. Now, it was a question that was good at what, especially women. Her father and stepmother haven't breathing space since Maddy was chosen to compete in the debate with Larsburg High School. The people at school and home felt engrossed with her preparation. Then the inevitable happened, Maddy was dismissed from the Demostheneans.(Demon)

Professor Miller laid down rules for the family after the death of their mother. Rule number one is: The family sticks together. No matter what. This rule Maddy applied in defending her sister when Zetta insulted her sister, Lou Emma. "I slapped her because of rule number one." Thus Mr. Grimes eqally used the school rule and suspended her from practicing in the debate in Larsburg.

At last, Maddy and Emma Lou engaged themselves in the campaign for Mrs. Biddle as the mayoress of Gloriosa. How it happened:

"When the man who had been a mayor of a town for

twenty years dies, it's as if the world has come to an end."

The funeral was held in the Gloriosa High School. Classes were dismissed for the day. Many of the students scattered for parts unknown, but Professor Miller insisted that the girls should attend, till the business was close for the day. Every preacher in town prayed.

Mrs. Biddle was Tommy's mother and together they came to the Millers to tell them about her contesting for the post of mayor. The Milers gave their consent and participated fully in the campaign. Many women admired such courage while most men did not fancy such intervention in what used to be dominantly men's affair. Jim Klugg was a good mayor as Professor Miller saw it, but there was a loop hole:

> "What do we get for it? One paved street,
>
> no real park, and the jail is a disgrace."

Professor Miller was the chairman of the Discipline Committee, at Eastern Kansas Classical College. (EKCC) The students often got caught up in one act or the other, so he went over to bail them and give them real hard one to do on the college. Mr. Meadows quarreled with his fiancé, Miss Baker over the issue. Miss Baker rushed over to report Mr. Meadows for allegedly threatening to cut off the engagement if she voted for Mrs. Biddle. They were to unite after finding Tommy's goat.

Mrs. Lavina Biddle was popularly in the town of Gloriosa for leading the demonstration against her opponent. She was called a native daughter. The day of the parade, the people of Gloriosa took to the street with different signs. The biggest read:

GOOD STREETS WILL MAKE GLORIOSA A BETTER TOWN. VOTE FOR THE GOOD STREETS" CANDIDATE LAVINA BIDDLE!

The tail end of the story relates the failure of people turning out to success. First, the demons won the debate despite, Maddy's absence. Mr. Grimes, the principal assembled all the students to announce the result and present the speaker for the success. Fortunately, for Maddy, Cal Conrad refused to take the honor and publicly declared Maddy as the brain behind what he presented at the debate. They were both after all accredited by the students, teachers, even Mr. Grimes. Maddy was reinstalled and her family was happy to see her filled with joy back. She decided to take part in the next year's debate.

Secondly, Mrs. Biddle was elected and she gave a party where she thanked her husband, son, Lou Emma and other people who aided her.

Thirdly, Lou Emma's dream of putting up a detective library in Gloriosa really came true, when Mr. Carrett gave out his big store to be used. Lou Emma was a symbol of love and care, to this extent, her jealousy for Zetta, being teamed up with Tommy which ended up with her concern when she eloped with Vance. She was published in the Silver Bugle, a daily newspaper. This sparked off her popularity and capability:"LOCAL GIRL WANTS LIBRARY!"

"Louisa Emmaline Miller, sophomore of Gloriosa High School wants a Library for Gloriosa with books to read, not to just study," Her story was related with her family background thus making her famous just like the mayor to be, Mrs. Briddle who endorsed the Reading Room as named by Miss Haspell.

JOYCE CAROL OATES:

BELLEFLEUR

A BLODSMOOR ROMANCE

MYSTRIES OF WINTERTHURN

Bellefleur is the first series of the Gothic Quintet that has been elaborately written. It contains the story of a set of people, their civilization and their language. The Gothic Quintet Hero is revealed by introducing her from the beginning of the novel.

The novel, Bellefleur, is an elaborate interlocking tales of six generations of the Bellefleur family and more than a century of the American history. By mingling actual historical events such as the war of 182, John Brown's abolitionist activities and building of the Erie Canal- with the mythical, one can read the eruption of all kinds of voices developing through the emergence of civilization.

Bellefleur is a notorious clan occupying a region by the mythical lake Noir. They are unique and eccentric group and are noted for all kinds of evil ways. Among them, are, millionaires, murders, spiritual leaders and whoever would benefit in the wrong way to benefit in the wrong way to benefit himself. Such are the variety of people living on this land. There are some static characters created by the author to drive her point of view home. The wealthy noctambulist who dies of a scratch, a young girl whose passion for her uncle can only be acted out on the scene and a brilliant boy scientist who has involved himself in the knowledge.

The major characters, Leah and her husband, Gedion are different pieces that need to be assessed accordingly. Leah is a young woman whose marriage is such pain in the neck. She gives her totality, loyalty, love and whatever while Gedion is full of dubious ways. He is a horse racer, gambler, flying planes and a womanizer.

The heroine, a girl so helpless like a leper named Germaine is the daughter of Leah and Gedion. She is handicapped and her growth is not with ease. She represents America, whose potentiality is misused and so helpless to curb the outrageous growth because everybody is involved. Germaine's birth is described in the novel:

>.......who is born with the lower half of her male twin

>Protruding from her abdomen, a female vampire.........

 A Bloodsmoor Romance:

T his is the second novel of the Gothic Quintet which contains the story of a rich man and his daughters. The five daughters are said to attain the marriageable age.

The characters are:

John Quincy Zhin

Phillipa

Malvinia

Octavia

Samanthia

Deirdre

John Quincy Zhin is an inventor, rich and popular in the town called Bloodsmoor Valley of Pennsylvania. Zhin has five daughters who are as filthy as a chimney but the grotesque image of their father is a coverage and an excuse to create scandal.

Phillipa is the first daughter, who is able to help herself with a man who proposes marriage, though in order to get herself freedom, she accepts. She behaves scandalously on her wedding night.

Malvinia is the second daughter who is seduced by men because of her beauty and helplessness. She disregards decency and embraces vices without avoiding it.

Octavia is the third daughter who is less rebellious, though not without the trait of innocence. She seems reserved and would have loved to be more inside than outside.

Samantha is the "brainy one "her father's great work she assists. She engages herself fully not caring whether it takes her time or it gives her little time for romance. All the time of work is not regarded by the other girls; to them she is wasting her precious time. She buried her head into her father's work with expected consequences.

Deirdre is the adopted daughter of Zhin thus making her the fifth. She is abducted in broad daylight in an outlaw bulbon of sinister black silken hire manned by an unidentified pilot.

The five daughters represent the various ethnic groups finding their way into America. They represent the five continents, Asia, Europe, Arabia, South- North America and Africa. The five daughters are the vision of American's formative years.

The novel is a blend of myth and history, from the arrival of the Europeans, the wars and the constitutions.

MYSTERY OF WINTERTHURN:

This is the third novel of the Gothic Quintet which deals with 19th century America. The detective hero and also the traditional hero, Xavier is confronted with three baffling cases of murder, all in Winterthurn. Xavier was born in Winterthurn, a place he regards as having all it takes for existing. There are factories for men to work, hotels for relaxation at weekends or evenings for the weeks. The town is also located amidst hills and rivers for surveying.

Xavier is captivated by the beauty of his place of birth that it takes quite some time before he associates the evils attributed to it. He joins the detective, a profession, he admires so much. In the course of his work, he is filled with the search for one murder or the other. He is happy to do anything that will make his work rewarding. This gives him time to slowly seek who has committed one offence or the other. In day and night, he walks to venues he suspects to have the mark of wickedness.

Xavier Kilgarvan as his full name is forced to come back to Winterthurn, to investigate the three murder cases. This investigation takes him into the ancestral mansion of the "rich" Kilgarvans. Here he meets his cousin Perdita.

Perdita becomes his hunt and thus the weakness in his detective work. Xavier realizes that most of the murders have taken place in Honeymoon Room by night. He is engaged in solving this crime but he is forced to acknowledge a scandalous family secret too shocking to be publicly revealed.

At age twenty, Xavier, climbing the ladder to the peak of his career, he investigates the murder of the local factory girls.

He catches the culprits and feels that other aristocratic Winterthurn citizen is guilty.

He becomes engaged to Perdita who remains a shadow throughout the novel. At the age of forty, the height of his fame, he withdraws from the profession of crime detection after the struggle to solve the mystery of the blood stained Bridal Gown.

Xavier is the archetype in this novel, however, he is able to solve triple cases and regain his long standing relationship with Perdita.

AKACHI ADIMORA EZEIGBO:

THE LAST OF THE STRONG ONES

HOUSE OF SYMBOL

CHILDREN OF THE EAGLE.

The novels of Akachi Adimora Ezeigbo are not only with traditional influence but reflect the occurrence of the sixties and seventies in the country of Nigeria. Interview with her on how she wrote these books, without mincing words, she claimed it was because she witnessed almost half of what she wrote. A woman of substance and caliber who could not get her eyes off the ills and dirt of the society is going to be honored in what I call the review of Akachi Adimora Ezeigbo's writing piece. Her best three novels which are trilogy of sequences of events. They are: The Last Of The Strong Ones, The House Of Symbol and The Children Of The Eagle respectively.

The follow up of her story witnessed the outcome of a war, Biafra civil war known as Nigerian Civil War. The story was composed in a book titled, The Children Of The Eagle. All the books will be reviewed and assessed like the others done earlier.

The Last of The Strong Ones:

The first of the trilogy, The Last Of The Strong Ones, was all about the traditions of a group of people known as the Igbos. She was able to select from the tribe in her story, societal norms as seen in The last Of The Strong and traditions of unequal formality with the people who are to carry them out as in The Children Of The Eagle.

The culture of the people is exposed through the events and individual activities throughout the story. Here is an excerpt reflecting disloyalty of an individual:

> Ejimnaka: Obuafo will meet tomorrow to discuss
>
> the stubbornness and uncooperative attitude of
>
> Okwara, the warrant chief………………..
>
> Okwara: Kosiri, will act, the people will talk.
>
> We must be careful. The women are not cooperating.

House of Symbols:

This novel notifies us about the continuation of two fortified figures. Okwara and Ejimnaka whose offspring eventually becomes one identity by marriage. Josiah Okwara cannot avoid the admiration of the young woman from the lineage of such powerful ardent controller of women of early Umuga.

It is the ancestral cause of Okwara family that debars his wife from getting pregnant. The House of Symbols signifies the two ancestral origins and claims- Okwara and Ejimnaka. Josiah represents his ancestor while his wife represents her ancestor. The two notable figures are making up their differences in their successors. The unity and peace which could not hold between the two are evidently established through the marriage of these young couple.

Mrs. Okwara, a rich bread baker but being deprived of procreation does not hesitate in helping the poor. Her dear husband who works in the local council is captivated by his wife's boldness and authority. Reincarnation of a dead one as prophesied by the prophetess depicts belief of a new religion which has replaced the old one.

The success of the marriage, the nomination of a good councilor and the death death of Josiah Okwara are the writer's method of creating characters worthy of emulation like Jane Austen, Pride and Prejudice and Sense and Sensibility.

Children of the Eagle

This is last of the trilogy in the Umuga Saga; the other two novels discussed above pave way for what we will read in this one.

"I told myself that I would go in search of a female

Okorigwe(the hero of Umuga) because I was convinced

she existed. If she did exist, then I must find her; I must

excavate and bring her to the limelight like her male

counterpart. But if indeed she didn't exist, then I would invent her- create her in my stories, in my writing(329).

The above extract from the novel summarizes Ezeigbo's aim- a search for and a recreation of a female Okorigwe, who signifies the heroic strength of women and a celebration of their indomitable spirit in the face of socio-cultural oppression. She achieves this aim by creating the story of a widow, Mrs. Okwara, nicknamed Eaglewoman, and her five proud daughters. Ogonna Okwara, Nduka is a teacher and a trader, while Amara Okwara Okoli is a university lecturer. Obioma Okwara Ebo is an evangelist, and Chiaku Okwara is a medical doctor.

The setting is her hometown, Umuga, in 1990. Children of the Eagle is a long novel of twenty-five chapters but the tripartite structural arrangement helps to hold the reader's attention to the end. Children of the Eagle is a novel social criticism and of epic dimension in its treatment of social issues. The social issues tackled by Ezeigbo include the criticism of religion as a tool of exploitation (155-156), the pervasiveness of bribery and corruption, especially among civil servants (156), communal conflicts in Umuga(252) and the horrifying effects of the Nigerian Civil War, especially on women(257).

Prominent among the issues recreated in the novel is the reality for gender inequality and female oppression that exists in Nigerian society.

Children of the Eagle is a feminist novel. She exposes the social conventions, cultural mores, and traditional practices that oppress and marginalize women, especially in Eastern part of Nigeria, as well as celebrates their struggle for freedom and survival. The community of Umuga, like other town in Nigeria, is patriarchal; the social conventions, cultural mores, and traditional practices are organized in favor of men. Preference for male children, the fact that too much importance is attached to male children, dehumanizing widowhood rite, the non-recognition of women's achievements, and incidents of rape and sexual harassment are addressed in the novel.

Umuga kinship structure is patrilineal and the community of the family lineage is through the male. Hence, the absence of a male child in the family of Josiah Obidiegwu Okwara(prior to the birth of Nkemdirim) is a warning of the extinction of the lineage, despite the presence of five daughters. His brother, Reuben, tactically reminds him that he has no heir when he asks Osai to sell to him his plots of land in Enyimba City. The importance attached to the male is made poignant in Igbo land. (Where Umuga is located) because of a land tenure system in which women are not allowed to inherit land. The reasoning behind this practice is that the female children soon get married, and it is abomination for a woman to carry her father's wealth to her husband's house.

The death of Osai Okwara, the head of Okwara family, exposes the family to the greed and avarice of neighbors who capitalize on his absence in order to encroach on their land. For instance, it is only after his death that the sons of Umeaku try to reclaim by force a piece of land that their father sold to Osai to solve a pressing problem Umeaku's "battalion of sons" is confident that there is "nobody" in Okwara's family to challenge their action since the grown children are women and the only son born into the family now lives in far away London.

The settlement of the land dispute is compounded by the fact that Ogunano Ezeala, the highest decision making body in the land, does not deal directly with women. When they finally come to demarcate the land, Pa Joel has to represent the Okwara family. It is then that the daughters of the Eagle realize that, "it is viewed as a misfortune to have a family populated by daughters" (75).

The birth of a son, Nkemdirim, into the family by one of the daughters, Obioma, is represented as the birth of hope, of continuity. The joy that welcomes his birth is one that obliterates the immoral nature of his origin. The joy of sadness of the family hangs on him. The news of his accident, for example, leaves Eaglewoman temporarily dead (unconscious).

 Her death symbolizes the future of the family (extinction of the family lineage) should anything happen to Nkemdirim. It is the threat to his life that requires the offensive "nluikwa" tradition, a tradition which, according to pa Joel, demands that:

> If Nkemdirim returns to his ancestors……then Amara(one
>
> of the daughters) should remain at home to perpetuate
>
> (their) father's name by producing a son or sons to

Inherit his vast property an d wealth in Umuga and other places(385).

Umuga culture is one in which people are valued not for their achievements but for their gender. Though Nkemdirim is not seen in the novel, his overriding presence is felt from the beginning to the end.

The "over-valuing" of the male gender means an "under-valuing" of the female. The gender bias is apparent in the event at which Umuga honors her citizens through the granting of chieftaincy titles and other awards. Women's contributions to the development of Umuga town are not recognized. Nnenne bemoans one such event where fifty citizens of Umuga are honored by Eze-Oha II in partnership with the Umuga Progressive and not even one of the recipients is a woman. Gender inequality is also inherited in the divorcees and their daughters when compare with the treatment of men and their sons. The fear of social stigma makes Ogonna, Eaglewoman's eldest daughter, stay in a bad marriage. The daughters of such women are no exception, either. " They say such girls cannot make happy homes"(126).

This discriminating social attitude makes marriage a cage that traps and enslaves women while men are given license to be dilettantes.

Widowhood rites are another of the crimes against womanhood discussed in the novel. Eaglewoman narrates her own terrifying experiences of these rites after the death of her husband, Osai. There is a compulsory three-day ritual lament of cockcrow, two weeks onslaught of the Umuda(kindred sisters of the husband) during which they are sumptuously fed amidst severe censorship, and one-year mourning period during which she was confirmed to her home(160-162).

The writer exposes the oppressive cultural traditions and social mores to the judgment of the audience. She portrays the degree of the inhumanity inherent in them by concentrating on the excruciating pain experienced by those at the receiving end of such cultural practices. The world of the novel is a world of don'ts for the women.

JANE OLAMIDE OLUBUNMI

BLACK MAIDEN

HERE AT LAST

THE EAGLE

The books of Jane Olamide Olubunmi are focuses on traditions and pre-colonial events. There are three books succeeding one another and reflecting chronological orders of events.

The Black Maiden:

This is a traditional and romantic tragedy which relates the story of a young girl sent as a gift to a king of Ilasa kingdom though her mission is to spy on the kingdom. The king of Ilasa is happy to receive such gift alongside with others. His total love for the new bride is evident in his neglect of the two other wives.

On the other hand, the new bride already renamed Duduyemi, is occupied with a mission imposed upon her by her father, who is the king of Ajele.

She equally returns the king's love and affection.

My Black maiden,

You are true ebony,

Your eye lashes are

like the feathers of an ostrich.

The relationship, though frowned upon by the elders who find out through the oracle that the new bride is a spy, they cannot make a decision.

Oloye Otun : The oracle clearly said, the

new bride is a spy.

In the palace:

Elders: The oracle has revealed the

new bride as a spy.

The king replies roughly:

King Adewale: Phoa! Abomination. My own

bride?

How dare you? This is conspiracy.

The king tries to confirm this, calls the high priest from Ipetu. The king drives the priest out of the palace when he reveals the same message through the oracle. Duduyemi is too cordial to the king to suspect as a spy.

The inquisitive, of the bride cannot be hidden, thus asking her maid to tell her about the kingdom.

> Duduyemi: Oh! I am sorry about that.
>
> What do you know about the kingdom?
>
> Eruku: I don't know much about it. Safi
>
> is the oldest slave in this palace.
>
> He knows a lot. He can tell you about
>
> this powerful kingdom.

Safi, the head slave hardly talks with slaves or king's wives. Duduyemi is disappointed until her fiancé comes searching for her. Having overheard in the market, where he sells the farm produce of his host, that Duduyemi, the new bride of the king, goes often with her maid to the river. The yam festival, brings them together, though Duduyemi is not aware of Aladeju, the fake name he gave his host, in the kingdom. Aladeju visits the riverside and soon gets himself known to Duduyemi.

This is done through the familiar song, which is the trend of knowledge to Eruku. Thus, on getting back to the palace, Eruku, the maid rushes to Olori Oriade, the first wife of the king and reports the scene at the riverside.

Eruku: My honour to you.

Olori Oriade: What is the matter?

Eruku: My mistress sang with a

young man at the riverside this morning.

Olori Oriade quickly goes to the king and makes it known.

Olori Oriade: Kabiyesi ooooo.

King Adewale: Anything? You look sad.

Olori Oriade: It is about your new bride.

King Adewale: What about her?

Olori Oriade: She is meeting a man at the riverside.

The king appoints two of his guards to monitor the movement of the new bride, Duduyemi. The day she plans to elope with Aladeju, is the day she gets caught and both of them are drag to the palace.

The king is very furious and lashes horrible words at Duduyemi.

King Adewale: Woe to you and the day you were born.

Woe to the one that gave you sucking.

Woe to the domain of your birth.

The heavens weep for the day of

your offshoot.

The moon shut the light that could

have brightened the earth.

The king orders that they should lock them up in the dungeon.

HERE AT LAST

This is a second book of the trilogy. It is the continuation of Black Maiden, which reveals the occurrence in the court yard and determination of Aladeju to elope with Otadiya. The guards are attentive and do not give room for any mischief.

Guard 1: Look, you must stop your noise.

The king has the upper hand.

Aladeju: I truly ask for water.

Guard I: You have your time of water

and food. It is not yet time for

the two yet.

On the part of Otadiya, she is not favored either.

Guard II: Woman, you are sober now.

Not a word has come forth

from your mouth.

Otadiya: Hmm, what am I to say?

Guard II: A word to give rest to your soul.

Eventually, Aladeju elopes with Otadiya which to the king's horror sends his warriors to pursue them.

King Adewale: Yes, that is why I have called

my warriors. Aladeju and Otadiya

must be found.

Warriors: Ye paripa.

King Adewale: They must be found, I know my

warriors are capable of finding

them.

Aladeju and Otadiya live among people in different villages along their journey back to Ajele, the kingdom of their birth. The warriors are not able to catch up with them. Therefore, the king orders the warriors should go to Ajele. There, they must destroy all that they find in it, even, the king, Otadiya's father that sent her down.

King Adepeju: Akoda! What is going on?

Chief warrior: The day of the evil doer stands out

like the sun.

King Adepeju: Alas! It is an attack.

The chief warrior strikes him with a machete. He dies while subjects and animals are killed. The houses are burnt and there is no evidence of lives or property anywhere.

Aladeju and Otadiya continue their journey towards the kingdom of their birth. They have resumed calling themselves in their real names. Osho and Asabi have given birth to a baby boy while residing in a village. Soon, they arrive in Ajele and to their surprise find an empty, stinking and horrible kingdom.

The Eagle:

The story is the sum up of the two previous books. In this story, the oldest man in the community tells his grandchildren the history of how the settlements around came to be under the same governance.

The story commences with the children sitting round an old man. The story he relates extends to how the settlements near the sea undertakes fishing as profession. Many come from the interior to purchase fish for personal use or sale. The people's way of life is related, such as marriage and the role of the eldest man in the entire family group.

Age group is important and they are the backbone of the community for strength both in the immediate family and community. A young man takes a wife and moves away from his family to start his own village or settlement. This is the routine and thus arises a large community out of it.

Wars are waged by powerful villages and conquered villages become vassals. The arrival of the white men at the coast creates fear and curiosity in the people. The men first see a white hand on the shore, fear grip them and they run back to the village. The second time, they see a ship like the shape of an eagle, they abandon their nets and run as fast as they can, screaming, the eagle has landed. Exploration of these white men into the interior, gives way to acquisition of slaves.

They go to the king by the coast and request for strong men to go back with them. The king does not ask about the purpose of the request but being offered gifts encourages him to go ahead with the task. The frequent demands pave way for the king ordering his warriors to wage constant wars on weak villages.

He gets in return, umbrellas, dazzling robes, fine royal shoes, scepters and other valuable goods. There comes a stop o the waging of wars and taking out of strong men as slaves. The oracle sends out his high priest to confront the king and warn of the vacuum he is creating. The king refuses to go ahead with the request of the white men. In the following visit, when they stretch out the gifts, the king rises up, shakes his head and retreats into his domain.

Dejectedly, the white men leave with their gifts.

DENOTATIONS AND CONNOTATIONS OF THE TITLES

JANE AUSTEN

PRIDE AND PREJUDICE:

This is directly the story of the Bennets family whose daughters are filled with prejudice and Mr. Darcy filled with pride, noticeable among the Bennets. Prejudice is a denotation of the attitude of the entire Bennets, which almost makes Lizzy loses Darcy.

The connotation of the novel is the attitude; the family engage themselves, judging others quickly.

EMMA

The denotation of the title is the name of the young girl that is narrated in the novel. Emma is the main focus in the novel.

The connotation is about the growing into adulthood of a young girl. The childhood of Emma contains relationships amidst relatives and friends. Her affection for Frank is part of her experience in growing up.

PERSUASION

This is a direct story about a father and his three daughters. Anne, the eldest daughter, the oldest daughter, who is the major character in the novel and is the persuasion of Harville to marry him that is revealed.

MANSFIELD PARK:

The denotation of the title narrates the activities in Mansfield Park. The title gives the impression of a name which is Mansfield. The connotation of the title is allegory of the Regency of England.

SENSE AND SENSIBILITY:

The denotation of this title explains the characteristics of the two sisters involved in the novel. Elinor's relationship with Edward, the former is more dominating. Marianne is the introvert, who guides her actions with thoughts. "Elinor for shame!" She disregards Elinor marrying because of wealth.

The connotation of the title can as well give us deeper meaning such as emotions and thoughts.

CHARLOTTE BRONTE

JANE EYRE:

Jane Eyre denotes the story of an orphan who, had life rough. The title implies the story of this orphan, whose name is Jane Eyre. The autobiography directly related by the author, contains early life of this determined young girl up to when she becomes the mother of a baby boy.

VILLETTE:

Villette is the name of a little town in England, thus denoting the name of a place but connoting the nature of any English town.

THE PROFESSOR:

This title is derived from the major character who happens to be a good and perfect teacher. The French version of "Teacher" is "Professor". William Crimworth, a renowned professor narrates. The connotation of the title is the perfect tutoring of Frances Evans Henry in learning English. It is obvious that the young man is a perfect professor as seen in all the schools he has taught.

MISS PERCY

This is another of Charlotte Bronte's biography of a little girl. The title denotes the name of this orphan, "Miss Percy". The connotation is the revelation of the agony of orphans as Miss Percy represents.

ALBERTA WILSON CONSTANT

DOES ANYBODY CARE ABOUT EMMA LOU?

Direct meaning of this title is the rhetorical question a fifteen year old asks herself when all attention is focused on Maddy, her junior sister alone both at home and school.

Indirectly, the title in a different dimension seems to be an accusation. It is ambiguous, giving us three dimensional meanings.

THE MOTORING MILLERS

Monitoring refers to mobility, which is exactly the author's motive. This title tells us without reading the novel that the Miller family has a motor. On the other hand, it means they were always going places in their motor.

JOYCE CAROL OATES:

BELLEFLEUR:

Bellefleur is a novel that tells of a people living in a town called by the title of the novel. Indirectly, it means a place in a period.

A BLOODMOOR ROMANCE:

This is a novel that has the description of five daughters of a man who find themselves in a different romance.

MYSTERIES OF WINTERTHURN

This novel denotes a young man, engaged in detective work and is faced with the horror of murder committed in Winterthurn, which is the place of his birth. The connotation is the revelation of his passion to fight crime and expose murderers.

AKACHI ADIMORA EZEIGBO

THE LAST OF THE STRONG ONES:

The title of the novel denotes the outstanding performance of a descendant of Umuga. Invariably, it shows none was to be seen as equal with him. The connotation reveals a clan that ceased to exist.

HOUSE OF SYMBOLS:

The denotation of the title is a remarkable house. It tells us about a unique sign attached to the house. Ironically, House of Symbols indirectly means a stagnant, impoverish life of a woman and search for continuity. The connotation of the title bears its resemblance to Mrs. Okwara coming to terms with identifying with her ancestors.

CHILDREN OF THE EAGLE:

The word "eagle", depicts a bird, therefore, rather than saying the siblings of the eagle, children is rather used. Grammatically, the title sounds incorrect but literarily, it is a suitable one, indirectly meaning descendants of Umuga. The connotation means the children of a woman nicknamed Eaglewoman.

JANE OLAMIDE OLUBUNMI

BLACK MAIDEN:

The title matches the young black princess. The denotation of the title is a young dark skinned girl. The connotation is the reflection of a traitor, the spy sent from another kingdom.

HERE AT LAST:

The denotation of the title is the fulfillment of a journey. The connotation is carrying out a mission successfully.

THE EAGLE:

The denotation signifies, the bird called eagle that swoops down to pick chicks. The connotation implies the carting away of Africans as slaves.

LITERARY ANALYSIS OF EACH TEXT

JANE AUSTEN

PRIDE AND PREJUDICE

Theme:

Pride means arrogance or self conceit. It applies to the same here. The word prejudice as it seems in this novel, indicates, in other words biased mind. The reflection of the topic appears in between Mr. Darcy and Elizabeth. All other relationships are quite cordial and expressive. Mr. Bingley and Jane were engrossed in intimacy so also Colins and Charlotte. Wickham absconding with Lydia, could be seen as unpreventable, yet it resulted into a marriage appreciated by both of them. Pride and Prejudice, therefore come forth from a relationship full of discrimination, false assertions and il-feelings.

Chapter xxxvi page 233 line 11 expresses Elizabeth's opinion of Mr. Darcy:

> He expressed no regret for what he had done
>
> Which satisfied her; his style was not pertinent
>
> but haughty. It was all pride and insolence.

Chapter xxxvi page 232 line 11 expresses Mr. Darcy's idea of apology to her. She thought:

> With a strong prejudice against
>
> everything he might say,............

Can we therefore say, Mr. Darcy is composed of the two ambiguous words, pride and prejudice. In no other part were these words used. Anchoring pride and prejudice he came stooping to ask Mr. Bennet for Elizabeth's hands in marriage.

EMMA:

It is the story of a young girl called Emma. Emma is the main focus in the novel. Each character is associated with a specific behavior as in Mr. Knightley, Mr. Woodhouse, Miss Smith, Emma's favorite. The three unique characters that Jane Austen uses to portray different attitudes are Emma, Jane Fairfax, and Harriet, Isabella also.

Emma seems to have different opinions about people; she detests Mr. Knightley and disregards Mr. Elton. A statement by one:

"Happy is the man who changes Emma for Harriet."

Jane Fairfax is very cold and snobbish towards everybody. Harriet is charming while Isabella is popular and enjoys it.

PERSUASION:

The characters in Persuasion are mixed up and comprises of the following: Mr. Elliot, a landlord and father of three daughters. Anne, the first daughter, once a friend of Fredrick and later gets engaged to Harville. Elizabeth, second daughter, who marries Charles Hater and Mary, who marries Captain Benwick. Other characters are: Lady Russell who wants there to be new Lady Elliot.

The theme relates to the predicament of Mr. Elliot who being in debt and his subsequent letting out the house for Mr. Fredric. It reflects the love lives of Mr. Elliot's daughter.

MANSFIELD PARK:

The theme is about ordination and it also connotes the Regency of England. The name Mansfield Park refers to a small place where most of the activities take place. The connotation of the theme is the merging of blending of civilization with countryside life. The Bertrams represent civilization while Fanny represents naivety. Thus, the accusation of the Bertram girls to see Fanny ignorant of some historical or geographical facts.

SENSE AND SENSIBILITY:

The theme is primarily about two sisters, Elinor and Marianne Dashwood. The former or earlier title of the novel was Elinor and Marianne. In another sense, Elinor means, sense, a reasonable person and Marianne, means sensibility, in support of Elinor's sense. Elinor has too much while Marianne is more sympathetic. Thus, the agony and grief which overpowered them at first on hearing their father's death. Austen's narration of the story gives us insight into the novel with money and love.

CHARACTERIZATION

Jane Austen portrays her characters uniquely. In all her novels, she made use of the following: personal description as in the three girls, Jane is the most beautiful of all; the reason Mr. Bingley sited her immediately on getting to Hertfordsshire.

Conversation of Mrs. Bennet with Mr. Bingley gives clue that Charlotte was not as beautiful as Jane.

EMMA:

Jane Austen presents Emma as a girl with reserved manner. She has different visions of the people she deals with.

PERSUASION:

Mr. Elliot, takes, the thoughts of his daughters highly. He is interested in one, Mrs. Russell knows which one. Anne is of two opinions, take Fredrick back or not. She marries Captain Wentworth and loves it. Elizabeth is Anne's sister and she takes delight in watching her activities. She volunteers to marry Charles Hauter in order to have access to him.

SENSE AND SENSIBILITY:

Elinor and Marianne are the major characters whose stories are related in full. The two sisters represent two identities.

Elinor is the sense of how to live her life. She concludes to marry Edward. Marianne says, "Elinor for shame!"

Climax: There is always a climax in Jane Austen's novel. In Pride and Prejudice, the climax is when the two girls, Jane and Elizabeth do not know their fate and have to hope for time to heal off their pain.

Elizabeth expects Mr. Darcy to show how he cares but always putting on pretence. Climax in Emma, is when the future of Emma cannot be decided. Frank Churchill fills her heart and does know it will not result into marriage. Yet her future is not decided. The author relates the climax in Mansfield Park when Fanny begins to fall in love with Edmund. Edmund's heartbreak over Miss Crawford is author climax.

Relating, climax in Sense and Sensibility, is the relationship of Elinor and Edward. Marianne's isolation is also a climax. Brandon asking Marianne to marry him is a relief indeed to the reader.

Comic Relief: The most enviable comic relief is when at two conservative times, the men, Mr. Bingley and Mr. Darcy ask the Bennet girls to marry them. It is a relief to Mrs. Bennet and the readers who thought that the men will not come back to the two girls, Jane and Elizabeth.

"It was an evening of common delight to them all.

The satisfaction of Miss. Bennet's mind gave a glow of

such sweet animation to her face, as made her look

handsomer than ever. Kitty simpered and smiled and

hoped her turn was coming soon. Mrs. Bennet could

not give her consent, or speak her approbation in

terms warm enough to satisfy her feelings,……………

Comic Relief in Sense and Sensibility is Elinor and Marianne getting married at the end of the story which is peculiar with Jane.

Comic Relief in Persuasion, Anne and her sisters, Elizabeth and Mary getting married happily. Anne is happy to be married to a sailor.

Comic Relief in Mansfield Park, Sir Thomas Bertram sees a good quality in Fanny and wants her to remain in Mansfield Park, even closer to Edmund.

CHARLOTTE BRONTE:

Jane Eyre, Villette, The Professor, Miss Percy

Theme:

Charlotte Bronte's writings are demonstrations about Race Empire and chromatic difference. Jane Eyre carries the name of the major character that captivated the attention of any of her readers. She claims the entire focus as soon as the reader lays hold on the novel. The novel is about a young girl who seems to be attracted towards a man whose wife was a lunatic.

She conforms to her ideology of keeping herself for the man who would make her happy. Fighting her cousin, who nearly raped her, was evidence of a young woman who would not want to be sexually abused.

The Professor is different, from Jane Eyre and Villette because of its masculine interaction except for the quiet romance between William and Frances Evans Henry.

Villette tells us about events in a little ancient English town. The theme is about a young orphan, who has lived with different kinds of people, Lucy, as she is called, has had

encounters with the people, she feels are one character or the other.

Characterization:

Charlotte Bronte portrays Jane Eyre as a helpless girl in childhood and adult. An orphan who lives in the midst of cruel relatives. Jane Eyre keeps her thought floating, thus

depicting her emotion and nature. Her nature is quite evident in her attitude to simple or biased occurrence.

In this novel, one sees a determined and self disciplined Jane as described by her.

The Professor is a novel that relates the autobiography of a man who engrosses himself in his teaching career, although it is a rough journey before getting to the peak of his career.

Villette has different characters portrayed carefully by exposing their characters. There is Mrs. Bretton with her snobbish behavior. Pauline, the young girl, Miss. Paul, Dr. Jone Miss Marchmont, Madame Beck, Mr. Horne, Paulina, Professeur Emmanuel and Lucy Snowe.

Lucy Snowe, the narrator, gives vivid description of all these people she comes across. She describes Madame Bek , the proprietress of the school, she has taught German as caring

and prudent but one that despises the closeness of her family which is evident in her withdrawal, if any wanted to embrace her.

Conflict:

There are conflicts in the three novels which can be seen within or without.

Internal Conflicts:

Jane Eyre struggling to overcome her love for Rochester.

Lucy Snowe's dejection for Professeur Emmanuel departure and the longing for his comeback as seen in The Professor.

The young hero's concern for Frances Evans Henry as portrayed in The Professor.

External Conflicts:

Jane Eyre's physical combat with her cousin who demands sex with her. Earlier on, her fight with her little cousins who has played pranks on her.

Lucy Snowe's struggle for a living and the quarrel with Mrs. Bretton in Villette.

And also, the hero's quarrel and hatred of Mr. William Crimson in The Professor.

Romance:

Romance in the novels of Charlotte Bronte can be noticed sometimes from the beginning after the introduction of the major characters all the way to the end. It does not stop there but often ends up in marriage. Thus giving us a clue that she appreciates the marriage industry.

Jane Eyre finally marries Edward Rochester, also Lucy Snowe having waited so long for Professeur Emmanuel ends up

wining his love. The young hero in The Professor patiently woos Frances Evans Henry, the teacher and her pupil.

Style:

Charlotte Bronte has a sleek style of introducing her characters as the first narrators as vividly noticed in Jane Eyre, Villette and The Professor. There are touches of nature and activities in all the sites she exposes to her readers. Description of Lowood in Jane Eyre, Bretton, and Villette in Villette and Belgium in The Professor.

Language:

Charlotte Bronte's expression and usage of words can be evidently seen. In Jane Eyre, she used simple and understanding sentences. Anybody, intellectual or vain, that can read and write should be able to comprehend the story effectively.

This excerpt tells of the servant's irritation:

> Jane: Master, how is he my Master?
>
> Am I a servant?
>
> Servant: No you are less than a servant,
>
> For you do nothing for your keep.........

Servant: There sit down and think over your

wickedness.

When Mrs. Reed punished Jane by locking
her up in the room, her simple statement of apology is
very clear:

Jane: Oh aunt! Have pity. Forgive me. I cannot endure it.

Let me be punished some other way! I shall be killed

if......

When Jane and Edward Rochester are about to get married:

Edward Rochester: Linger, he says, my brain is on fire with

Impatient and you tarry so long!

He further says, seeing her in the

wedding gown:

"fair as a lily."

Jane's news to marry Mr. Rochester is received
without surprise.

Jane: Mary, I have been married to Mr. Rochester

this morning.

Mary: Have you Miss? Well for sure!

Mary's husband is not surprised either:

I telled Mary how it would

be. I wish you joy Miss.

Jane: Thank you John.

Villette, is not different either, Paulina brooding over
her papa:

Paulina: Papa; my dear papa!

Professeur Emmanuel's commendation of Lucy as a good
protestant:

Professeur Emmanuel: Protestantanism in you.

I own its severe charm. There is

something in its ritual. I cannot

receive myself, but it is the sole

creed for Lucy.

Lucy rejoices over her success:

Lucy: My school flourishes, my house

is ready, I have made him a little library……….

ALBERTA WILSON CONSTANT

DOES ANYBODY CARE ABOUT LOU EMMA MILLER?

THOSE MILLER GIRLS

THE MOTORING MILLER

Theme:

Those Miller Girls is a novel exposing the life style of an average American family. Professor Miller, his wife and two daughters are engrossed in their daily activities and the love bounding them together is very obvious. The death of Mrs. Miller is a turning point in the life of the Miler Girls when their widower father marries Miss Kate and keeps the new 1911 Great Smith polished and rolling about the country.

This novel is sequel to Those Miller Girls.

Does Anybody Care About Lou Emma? Is the continuation of the Motoring Millers. The novel reveals the enthusiasm and exuberance of small- town America in the early part of the twentieth century. A woman running for the mayor of Gloriosa. Some people think Mrs. Biddle's campaign is an outrage. Lou Emma Miller thinks it's one of the best things to have happened in Kansas since woman's suffrage, then idea of a library.

CHARACTERIZATION:

The three novels are filled with rich characterizations and wit. Those Miller Girls gives us the description of each character: by virtue of appearance and speech. Professor Miller is presented as an intellect of history, Roman History whose family share in this knowledge too. Although Professor Miller is indebted in his profession, he devotes himself to his matrimony too. He helps Mrs. Miller, his wife in raising up their two girls. The little town of Auden, they live reflects the nature of the environment.

The Motoring Millers includes minor characters whose attitude equalize or contradict the Millers. The Millers seem to be the easy going type. Despite, Professor Miller owning the Great Smith, the first auto elegant enough for such educated couple. Professor Miller who is better known as a teacher of Greek and Roman History or as the man who owns the Great Smith, an auto manufactured in Topeka.

Does Anybody Care About Lou Emma Miller? Contains outstanding characters such as Lou Emma Miler, the untouched girl both in her family and at the school. Her physical appearance is known only when compared with

Tommy, her boyfriend as slightly shorter than him and freckles on his face. Maddy is another character noted for

her beauty and popularity for brilliancy. Zetta Colby is known for waywardness which irritates both students and teachers.

Mrs. Biddle's character is revealed more in her control over her husband and son, Tommy. The ardent discipline she imposes on her son has enriched Tommy good moral. Professor Miller, Miss Kate, Barney, Miss Haspel, Miss Baker and others like Mr. Grims. Mr. Hollins, even the animals,-Swish and Old Polly.

Conflicts:

Internal Conflicts

The novel introduces us to the struggle for recognition in Lou Emma Miller's thought. "Maddy's pretty. Prettiest' n than me. Prettier of all when she's like this." She further says: "All right. She was boiling to say nothing was alright."This is in response to Miss Kate's question. "How're things at school? Not lessons, just......things?"

There is the internal struggle over Tommy and Zetta Colby.

External Conflicts

Maddy fighting Zetta over her utterance about Lou Emma is one.

Comic Relief

There is a great relief when Maddy is given recognition when the Demons won the competition.

The whole town of Gloriosa becomes satisfied and happy when Mrs. Biddle won the election to become the mayor. At last Lou Emma Miler realizes she has been falsifying stories against Tommy by connecting him with Zetta.

Climax:

Three consecutive peaks are noticed in Does Anybody Care About Lou Emma Miller? One, the realization of the local library. Two, the election of the mayor of Gloriosa. Three, the relationship.

Soliloquy:

The many occasions which warrant speeches erupting from the character in Does Anybody Care About Lou Emma Miller? Is noticed from the beginning of the novel in Lou Emma Miller. "Did Tommy Biddle notice Zetta Colby's ankles?" "Does anybody care about Lou Emma Miller?

Pathos: The three books of Alberta Wilson Constant are filled with pathos. The death of Mrs. Miller in the Motoring

Millers. The sympathy of the neighbors and the dejection of Professor Miller.

The death of the mayor of Gloriosa, Mayor Klugg, arouses pity in the people both young and old.

"When a man who has been mayor of a town for twenty years dies, it's as if the world has come to an end."

The death of the characters of Alberta Wilson Constant is often reported suddenly which leave the readers astonished.

"Papa says Maddy has a natural talent for debate,

and if she works at it in high school, when she goes to EKEC.."

There are rhetoric questions which often leave readers what to expect next. "Does anybody care about Lou Emma Miller?

Style:

Surprisingly, the author has gracefully presented each character according to age groups and status. The school children mentioned in the three novels give us insight into how they interact among themselves. There is obvious recognition of rules and regulation imposed on the children in school. Maddy, Lou Emma, and Zetta's prompt dismissal

from after engaging in physical combat reveals the thorough discipline children obtain from the school. The author has also exposed the love in family set up as in the Millers. The society frowning on misbehavior and women recognition as read about Zetta and Mrs. Biddle.

Language:

The author of the three books used in this doctoral thesis, has exposed readers to factual of life, by demonstrating simple English and direct sentences. Dialogues are not farfetched. Listen to the dialogue between Lou Emma and Adelaide:

"How d' ya like it? Adelaide twirled on the step.

"It's nice" Lou Emma despised herself for being a ninny. Reported speeches are also noticed.

JOYCE CAROL OATES

Bellefleur

A Bloodsmoor Romance

Mysteries of Winterthurn

Theme:

Bellefleur is the first of the Gothic myths of Joyce Carol Oates. It relates the series of interlocking tales of six generations of the Bellefleur family.

A Bloodsmoor Romance is her version of the 19th century romance steeped in Victorian and told by demure, virgin narrator. It is an ingenious blend of myth and history and provides us with a singular vision of American's formative years.

Mysteries of Winterthurn deals with the 19th century America. The detective hero, Xavier Gilgarvan is confronted with three baffling cases, all in Winterthurn, place of his birth.

CHARACTERIZATION:

The characters in each of the Gothic Myths erupt from the readers sympathy or condemnation. In Bellefleur,

Germaine's birth represents the heroine of the novel. Leah, her mother and Gideon, her father, are the symbols of decadence of a society.

Bloodsmoor Romance is filled lace, sweet songs, revealing the daughters of Zhin who are the major characters of a novel.

Traditional Heroes:

Mysteries of Winterthurn has more of a traditional hero than a displayed character. Xavier is obliged to come across series of murders in Winterthurn. The shocking effect of all the murders taking place in the place of his birth, Winterthurn. Perdita is seen as a relief to all that could have brought frustration to Xavier. Xavier, being able to solve the triple murder cases and a clue to his long standing relationship with Perdita makes him the traditional hero of the story.

Anachronism:

The three or rather the Gothic Quintet is derived from the Gothic Tales which was established in England in the late

18th and 19th centuries respectively. Each novel is mixed up with archaic and eccentric features.

Burlesque:

A Bloodsmoor Romance reveals the ridicule of the three daughters of Zhin. They represent America and modernity.

Stereotype:

Perdita is an unchanging character in the novel "Mysteries of Winterthurn. One realizes Xavier in total control of the relationship.

Scream of consciousness:

Xavier seems to flow in thought throughout the story. His concern over mass murder combined with his deeply thought affair exposes him more to the reader.

This literary style is also in Bellefleur, here, many occurrences are revealed. Germaine's mother constantly thinking about her husband and his behavior, the author tries to approximate the chaotic nature of unorganized mental activities.

Symbols:

The author uses the titles of the Gothic Quintet to drive her message home. The Bellefleur family symbolizes erotic nature of America at the time of her writing. A Bloodsmoor Romance gives the impression of danger and death which are very obvious in the novel. In the Mysteries of

Winterthurn, Xavier and Perdita are symbols of innocence and love. In order to avoid total depression caused by death tolls in the novel, Xavier and Perdita help elevate the effect on the readers.

Languages:

Surprisingly, the language used in the Gothic Quintet is simple direct unlike most thrillers. The first novels of the Gothic Quintet are interestingly fascinating, claiming the totality of the readers.

Romance:

 She includes in the Gothic Quintet, romance which is conspicuous. Each of Zhin's daughters is exposed to different love affair in A Bloodsmoor Romance. Germaine in Bellefleur, falling in love with a young unequal man. Xavier and Perdita in the Mysteries of Winterthurn, proves the nature of Joyce as somebody who values love just like Jane Austen.

Style:

She has been able to present her writings to the readers, her thoughts and purpose of writing the Gothic Quintet. The qualities and characteristics of her characters have distinguished her works from others. Her linguistic choices implicitly and explicitly have conveyed her cast mind, her temperament, her taste, her values- in short, herself as she wishes us to believe.

AKACHI ADIMORA EZEIGBO:

THE LAST OF THE STRONG ONES

HOUSE OF SYMOLS

CHILDREN OF THE EAGLE

Theme:

The Last of the Strong Ones relates the ancestral tribe of a lineage of people who lived in the Eastern part of Nigeria. A settlement called Umuga and the surrounding villages. The culture and traditions of this clan is Akachi's focus. The House of Symbols gives us insight into descendants of the Umuga clan and the subsequent consequence of tradition in the emergence of colonialism. The young woman in this novel put herself in a position of freedom fighter. She suffered the agony of having children after marriage. Her visitation to the prophetess and prophecy of giving birth by bringing alive the dead was not immediately embraced by her. Carrying out the prophetess' ritual actually enhanced her ability to get pregnant.

Children of the Eagle is about Mrs. Okwara, a widow and a mother of five daughters and presumably, a son. She went through the agony of male chauvinism, being denied access to her husband heritage because she had no male child. The birth of a son, Nkemdirim into the family by one of the daughters, Obioma, depicts, continuity and peace after such trauma of scorn from men and women alike.

Characterization:

The characters in the trilogy suffer a bit physical descriptions. All that is read about them is the characteristic features indicating behaviorism. In The Last of the Strong Ones, behavior of the men and women could be accounted for.

House of Symbols and Eagle Woman have characters portrayed with delicacy. Symbolically, Mrs. Okwara became to be known as Eagle woman because of her ability to stand the test of time.

Children of the Eagle refers to children of the powerful one.

Conflicts:

Revolts of women could be read in the second trilogy. They wanted their differences solved. At this prime age in the era when traditional and cultural beauties were evident, women were not kept away from ruling power but there was nomination in the village, opting out a head who controlled the women. She was all out to make sure everything went well among them. Women also helped in the care of men all around. Men took wives left over by the dead ones or unfortunate

ones. Some women at the time had different thoughts of their interactions or short comings in the face of tradition.

Internal Conflicts:

This is remarkable in Mrs. Okwara who constantly lived in fear of not having children since her marriage to Josiah

Okwara, evident in House of Symbol, Eagle Woman's torment of an absence of a male child in the family is an outstanding evidence of an internal conflict even when Nkemdirim had an accident. She became obsessed with fear of losing the only hope for securing the family inheritance.

Symbols:

The first novel of the trilogy also relates fascinating events. It is glaring, the use of symbols to denote literary meanings. House of Symbols, symbolizes the family trend. Eagle in Children of The Eagle symbolizes

strength.

Climax:

The climax in The Last of the Strong Ones is when the people are afraid of losing the war to Kosiri.

The climax in House of Symbols takes two parts. One, when Mrs. Okwara is skeptical about when she will get pregnant. Two, people are so conscious of who will become the counselor.

The climax in Children of the Eagle is seen when Eagle woman do not know what will become of her in the absence of a male child. There is that rising and falling episodes in this novel. Nkemdirim's accident marks the thought of survival

Tragedy:

There are evidently, cases of tragedy in the Umuga Saga. They have come in the form of death. In The Last of the Strong Ones, Ejimnaka dies from falling off the tree. In the House of Symbols, Josiah Okwara loses his life after an illness, hard combat.

Traditional Heroes:

The Umuga Saga has the traditional heroines as order of preference. Ejimnaka is the heroine of Umuga who fights her way through by displaying recognition of women in the community. Mrs. Okwara, wife of Josiah Okwara, is the heroine in House of Symbols. She makes herself available to the people all around her and reinforced the election of a candidate suitable for the post of a counselor.

Eaglewoman, known as Mrs. Okwara, continues her dominance as the heroine in Children of the Eagle.

Style:

Akachi Adimora Ezeigbo's style is pure narrative method and plain dialogue effect. She uses symbols and idioms to stress her point. The songs are larded with poetic qualities.

> The happy child swings
>
> from branch to branch
>
> agile like a money
>
> nimble like a monkey
>
> nimble like a squirrel
>
> on withered branch
>
> the world as a pleasant place,
>
> let the enemy be at a retreat
>
> there is no place for him here.

Language:

The language is simple and direct and is meant to ensure that the audience understands the important, urgent message so that they can act on it. The language is touching, carrying the message of the novel as smoothly into the deepest crevices of the mountains The language is also rendered more pleasurable by the use of certain devices that evoke clear, distinct images. Prominent among the devices is the use of symbols. Akachi Adimora Ezeigbo is really in love with symbols. There is a pervasive use of the eagle as a symbol of strength, the kind of strength women need to withstand and overcome the cultural oppression and to reform the society. There are also the symbols of the wall gecko as the predator (man) and its prey at the victim (woman). The first and third person points of view are used. The first person point of view makes most of the incidents confessional and hence, authentic and captivating, as the reader follows the characters into the innermost part of their past and present lives.

The novel is not without fault. Its main weakness emanates from its epic nature. The issues covered are so vast that sometimes the story seems to move away from the focus of the novel. Some of the incidents even seem to assume a life of their own life.

However, total disintegration is checked by the fact that the novel is cast in the form of an enquiry, a form of data collection, for the writing of a biography of the family. In the end, Akachi Adimora Ezeigbo succeeds in recreating a female Okorigwe in the lives of Eaglewoman and her five daughters, who are set up models for feminist struggle. The message is clear: "Let the eagle soar high, and her children higher still."

JANE OLAMIDE OLUBUNMI

BLACK MAIDEN

HERE AT LAST

THE EAGLE

Theme:

Black Maiden relates the events of the earliest time of this nineteen century in a popular kingdom of a tribe known as Ijesa. A king sends his daughter as a gift to another king in Ilasa. This means she is bestowed to the king as a bride.

Eventually, the oracle proclaims her as a spy. The king who has taken likeness to the bride disagrees and dismisses all the elders that have brought the report.

Here At Last is the continuation of Black Maiden. The story in the book, tells us how the bride of the king elopes with her fiancé from the prison yard.The king's warrior rampage and search cannot locate them. Eventually, Osho and Asabi, arrive in the kingdom, alas, it has been razed down by Ilasa warriors. Determinedly, Osho rebuilds the kingdom and his son reigns in his stead.

The Eagle is the conclusion of the story, which tells of the kingdoms formed by Adewale, Adeosho and others being turned into haven of slaves trafficking to the white man's land.

Characterization:

The writer has presented her characters in the eye of the beholder. Duduyemi in **Black Maiden** is seen as a young beautiful black girl with eyelashes fluffy and neck long and tender. Olori, the first wife of king Adewale, seems to be light skinned and beautiful but whose beauty cannot be matched up to the new bride. Fabunmi is regarded vain, who has always been in the background, although her physical appearance is not related. She is happy to have Olori replaced who has been mocking her before the arrival of Duduyemi. King Adewale, who is being introduced in the story running away from the wrath of his elder brother, Aderopo because their father has declared him succession to the throne. He later becomes a king in the settlement he has found.

Aladeju, the fiancé of Duduyemi, a young, agile and handsome man as proclaimed by Duduyemi, warning the young girls of Ilasa to stay away, gives us a clue that her heart remains with him.

The Eagle features diverse characters in which none is protagonist or antagonist. The age group shows the important role young ones play in the society. The king, the warriors, the white men and the slaves, enable us to know the conclusion of the story and where the orator is heading to.

Episode:

The trilogy is a continuous story that links us from one end to the other, that is, pre-colonial to colonial era. It is obvious that the first two books are in episodes. The first part of

Black Maiden relates the episode of Adewale's decision to leave his father's kingdom since his elder brother, Aderopo refuses to allow him to mount the throne as declared by their father before his death.

Another episode is when Adewale becomes the king and a bride is bestowed to him from the king of Ajele. Thus it continues to when Duduyemi is suspected to be a spy and lastly being caught with a young man.

Here At Last has the plan and escape of Aladeju and Duduyemi as the introductory episode. King Adewale getting to know and subsequent search is the second episode. The third episode tells us the activities and encounters of Aladeju and Duduyemi during the journey back to their kingdom. The forth episode is the total destruction of Ajele kingdom and its rebuilt by Osho.

Flashback:

In **Black Maiden**, Adewale reminisced on the secret of his succession to the throne as authorized by his father before his death.

> Onward ever, backward never. How can he become
>
> the king?
>
> Did father not call me and told me to become the
>
> king?
>
> No, he would not hear of it.

Protagonist:

King Adewale is the protagonist in the book. He maintains the posture from Black Maiden to Here At Last, whereby he did not suffer defeat.

Aderopo is the first antagonist in Black Maiden. Aladeju and King of Ajele are equally antagonists.

Soliloquy:

King Adewale in Black Maiden soliloquies when he is leaving his father's kingdom. He also soliloquies when the report of Duduyemi is brought to him, and when the guards go in search of Duduyemi , etc.

Can anyone refuse such adorable gift?

Duduyemi, laments over the suspicion of the people.

I must be careful, people are watching.

Climax:

In Black Maiden, the climax is when Duduyemi is suspected as a spy. The elders, the declaration by the oracle and confirmation by the priest of Ipetu. They are and the suspense paves way for uncertainty of what would be the result of the oracle's demand for the purification of the palace.

Climax in Here At Last is the suspense of Otadiya and Aladeju, whether they will be found and returned to the king. It lingers on until the break off, when he warriors invade Ajele kingdom and the return of the couple.

The Eagle places the reader in dilemma, the white hand on shore, the eagle-like ship and the white men are the peak.

Figurative Language:

There are figurative expressions in Black Maiden and Here At Last. The king full praise of his bride Duduyemi:

My black maiden, you are true ebony,

Your eye lashes are like the feathers of an ostrich...........

Duduyemi cannot hide her love for her fiancé:

My beloved is mine and I am his………

Thou whom my heart loveth……as expressed by Duduyemi depicts true love.

Condemnation of Duduyemi's act and betrayal by king

Adewale are expressed in proverbs, thus giving us insight into the depth of Duduyemi's offence.

The figurative language used in Here At Last, at the tail end and it is quite remarkable.

Language:

The language of the author is simple but complex because of the proverbs and idioms used. The word "thou" takes a reader back to the barbaric era. The three successive books termed "the trilogy" are proof of the pre-colonial era where villages and kingdoms sprouted up in terms of power and wealth. Black Maiden and Here At Last tend to represent human's quest for power and fame.

Style:

A perfect style of connection is realized in the presentation of the trilogy which triggers off, the interest of the readers. Getting abreast with episodes, thus, linking them to one occurrence or the other. There is the sequent of interesting events, that make the stories interesting and unique.

METHODOLOGY

The method of writing y each author differs greatly and there is cordial communication to the readers. All the female authors expand their readers, knowledge of literary forms, terms and techniques. They express their main objectives to their readers and clear understanding is received. An author like **Jane Austen** had created cross circular connections with her readers. She portrayed the characters in all the novels used in this thesis as vivid as real people. Lizzy in Pride and Prejudice, Miss Bates in Emma, Mrs. Norris I Mansfield Park, Anne Elliot in Persuasion and Elinor and Marianne in Sense and Sensibility. All of which have distinct characters displayed from indifferent, self centered, tyrannical, loving and respectful according to the order of preference.

Charlotte Bronte created first singular narrator to express her stories. In Jane Eyre, she often gets a break to remind them(the readers) that she is still the narrator, thus saying.....”Dear reader,” Lucy Snowe in Villette proved her story from the beginning to the end. The young teacher is the spectator of all that happened in the novel, The Professor. All the characters such as Mr. Reuter, Mr. Crimworth, Mr. Edward Crimsworth, Mr. Pelet, Amelie Mullenberg and Frances Evans Henry to mention a few. Mr. Crimsworth, a stingy, selfish and wicked creature so he is to the young narrator who has taken appointment with him.

Pelet, who calls him, "Mon fils" is also an irritated man and Frances Evans Henry, the helpless young girl are all the character creating of Charlotte Bronte.

Alberta Wilson Constant is the narrator in all her novels, except presenting reported speeches to buttress her points to the readers.

Those Miller Girls is narrated the readers, revealing domestic life and extra-curriculum of the family. The display of automobile is the astonishment of owning a vehicle at the time. Does Anybody Care About Lou Emma Miller? Completes the story of the Millers. Lou Emma and Mrs. Biddle are victims of inferiority complex. Lou Emma to her sister Maddy and Mrs. Biddle to Tim Moss.

Joyce Carol Oates has used the descriptive method. Relating the …It was many years ago on the dark, chaotic(nearly twelve months before her birth), on a night in late September……."or The virgin in the Rose-Bower".

Akachi Adimora Ezeigbo expressed the trilogy in epic form. She has used literary devices such as symbols and images. In The Last of the Strong Ones, proverbs and idioms are immensely used. The House of Symbols claims creative words which suit each event. The Children of the Eagle signifies upholding strength and overcoming."Eagle" as used by the author means strength.

Jane Olamide Olubunmi has narrated the three books with poetic words supporting. Black Maiden has the major characters featuring prominently throughout the book. Duduyemi is praised by king Adewale:

> My black maiden, you are true ebony,
>
> your eye lashes are like the feathers of
>
> an ostrich..........

Duduyemi wading off the young girls of Ilasa from her spouse that has come looking for her is all composed in poetic form:

> Women of Ilasa, stay away,
>
> my beloved is mine and I am is.
>
> His banner over me is love.........

Here At Last continues the poetic form by putting into the minds of the readers, nature of events. Aladeju vows to recreate the crumbled kingdom:

> I will create yet a kingdom, surpassing Ilasa and reign
>
> with might. My son, Adeoye shall reign in my stead.

The Eagle is a complete narration, with prologue opening the story and epilogue ending it. The Eagle reveals the village set up of a tribe and all it takes to be a full member, thus the age group issue. There is the men at the sea fishing and the trade in fish by women which show the occupation of the people. It is at the sea side that the fishermen come across the white men that later become slaves trafficker.

The author has been able to bring to the limelight the original source of slavery. This originates from the waging of wars and capturing slaves to work on the king's farms.

Ironically, the slaves acquired by the white men are to be exported to work on the farm as one of the white men indicates at the tail end of the story. The dialogue below indicates the primary aim of the traffickers:

> STRANGE WHITE MAN : The hour has come
>
> for son of men to move on.
>
> STRANGE WHITE MAN II : And when sons of
>
> God shall have more money.
>
> STRANGE WHITE MAN : Not only money, but
>
> have more money and a
>
> full grown plantation.
>
> STRANGE WHITE MAN I : Are you going to
>
> involve yourself in that stuff?

Comparative study of the texts of the selected female authors

Common views:

All the female writers selected in this thesis are feminists. They focus their objectives in realizing female upgrading and fairness. It is quite obvious that they are all fighting against human degradation and women abuse. In one manner or the other, they have been able to present their characters to the best available exposure for human consumption and reality.

Jane Austen, in her novels focused on behaviorism, in which to perpetuate the order of ethics in its true sense. Pride and Prejudice reveals the value of marriage and the craze for it. Sense and Sensibility is another of her novel where knowledge is required, a literate woman is accessible and respected.

One could also link up **Charlotte Bronte** with her novels of maltreatment of orphans and abuse of women's right and privilege. Jane Eyre is a valuable novel which reveals the predicament and helplessness of women in the face of trials. This is evident in Jane and the widow, Mrs. Reed. In her other novels, Frances Evans Henry in The Professor and Lucy Snowe, Villette are celebrates of despair and dejection.

Alberta Wilson Constant is not only writing on the issue of women ostracisation but child abuse. The novels presented in this literary works have expressed the need for women participation in politics and holding posts that have been dominated by men. Thus, acclamation of the women of Gloriosa even young girls like Millers assisting in the campaign.

Joyce Carol Oates is the contemporary of Alberta Wilson Constant in that she has equally written about America, using the feminine gender to convey her message of the decadence of America. Her first three consecutive novels, Bellefleur, A Bloodsmoor Romance and Mysteries of Winterthurn are all part of the Gothic Quintet.

Akachi Adimora Ezeigbo in all the novels she has written is concerned about women being recognized in the society. House of Symbols contains similar occurrence like Does Anybody Care About Lou Emma Miller? In the former, Mrs. Okwara participates in the election of a fair counselor, which only men take part. Children of the Eagle is an extention of women abuse and condemnation. Eaglewoman with her children face the ordeal of uncivilized tradition.

Jane Olamide Olubunmi has also written about women in a different dimension which has to do with men. In Black Maiden, there is condemnation of one woman at the expense of another. Thus, king Adewale has to condemn his two wives to give attention to the new one, Duduyemi. A female character has represented the incredible act of man. Duduyemi in Black Maiden is an epitome of bravery as

Eaglewoman who faces the ordeal of claiming the family land. Duduyemi eloping with Aladeju shows the totality of her boldness.

Different views

The authors have presented their stories in different dimensions. One is focusing on societal norms as in all

Jane Austen's works. Pride and Prejudice depicts morality, decency is her watch word. Arrogance and negligence found in Mr. Darcy and Lizzy noticing these two in herself, both Austen condemns.

Charlotte Bronte was able to account for damp spirit, which came in form of sorrow and dejection, thus Jane Eyre's loneliness and dejection. Lucy Snowe's weakness and frustration in Villette and Frances Evans Henry in The Professor portrays uncertainty. Alberta Wilson Constant used the matrimony to convey her message. The three concurrent novels Those Miller Girls, The Motoring Millers and Does Anybody Care About Lou Emma Miller? Are evidently home affair exposition in one piece.

Joyce Carol Oates had been able to present a remarkable, on-going portrait of America life, many years ago in the dark chaotic unfathomable pool of time. This signifies emotional experience which could not be avoided; rather, the narration should ease off the depression it has brought.

Akachi Adimora Ezeigbo proved her worth by utilizing traditions of Umuga to reveal her intentions. The women she produced in the three novels could not have performed well without being attached to the traits of their traditions. Condemnation of such traditions through her characters, is hiding behind the mask to make her objective, a reality. All the same, the Saga has provided good forum for this.

Jane Olamide Olubunmi, focused on claiming a hero out of heroine, thus presenting Duduyemi a female spy is equalizing women with men. The third of the trilogy where there are male dominance in control of power is to reveal the fierce nature of males in the tradition she wrote about. The silence of women and their major roles as, brides, housewives and sellers is to show where they belong in the society.

BIOGRAPHY OF EACH FEMALE WRITER

BRITISH WRITERS

JANE AUSTEN

Jane Austen was born in1775 in Steventon, Hampshire, England. She lived at a time, when a lady was happy to have no history, and before the camera was invented. Jane, though descriptions of her by friends was said to be as graceful with laughing eyes and regular features, loving a dance and wearing uncommonly pretty clothes, finding fun in almost everything, but never poking fun at anybody. She was always writing her novels, which she herself compared to scraps of ivory on which the design is painted with a tiny brush. Right in the family living room, she sat writing and whenever a visitor entered, she kept aside the paper and engaged herself in sewing or embroidery. In Steventon, her father was rector; she went with the family to Bath, when he retired. When her father died, she first went to Southhampton and then to the village of Chawton in the South of England, till her health, gently and too early declining, made it necessary to go to Winchester for medical aid. There Cassandra, her sister closed her eyes after long pain borne with unfailing sweetness. She laughed to the last, in her own delightful way. It seems Jane Austen herself was all unconsciously drawing something very like her own portrait in Lizzy, and of one thing, in Jane, the eldest Miss Bennet, the essential traits of character are those of Miss Austen's sister, Cassandra.

Almost all her written words are recorded in a letter that says: "You will find Captain –ma very respectable, well-meaning man, without much manner, his wife and sister all good humor and obligeness, and I hope(since the fashion allows it) with rather longer petticoats than last year."

Jane Austen was a true artist at creating proposal scenes, and she must have had several on her own account, but none of them was ever accepted. She remains to us "dear delightful Jane" with no other name than the one she started with.

Six novels of Jane Austen are printed in five volumes and these are the five that anybody would like to read on a desert Island.

CHARLOTTE BRONTE was born in1816 and died in 1855 in England. She was the eldest of two other sisters who were also writers. Emily Jane Bronte was born in1818 and she died in 1843. Anne Bronte, the youngest of them was born in 1820 and she died in 1849. The three sisters wrote extensively on fiction. Emily Jane and Anne were fascinated by their sister's writings that they picked up writing too.

Charlotte Bronte loved to personify her writings thus the single name title of her novels. Jane Eyre, Miss Percy and

Shirley were novels that are autobiographies respectively. She was fully engrossed in her writings that little room was given for leisure. Most of the fascinating events in her novels were occurrences or personal experiences.

Patrick Bronte, Charlotte's father equally encouraged his daughters to write and assist publishing their works. Charlotte was such a quiet woman who enjoyed free privilege of privacy. One could easily notice the manipulation of her characters from the beginning of the self related style to the end. Jane Eyre and The Professor are master piece of perfect autobiographies.

The following are popular novels of Charlotte Bronte.

Jane Eyre

The Professor

Miss Percy

Villette

Invariably, she wrote at the time literature was becoming the essential issue. This is classified into the Victorian Literature and she was the first woman to write effectively during the reign of Queen Victoria. This bravery paved way for other female writers who felt weighed down by the female criticism of the time.

Her novel, Shirley demonstrates her white demonstration about races and chromatic difference, which are evident in her characters.

Charlotte Bronte's husband, A.D. Nicholls had to publish The Professor, a novel which he believed was not concluded, but could be the follow up of Villette.

She died in 1855 after a long deterioration of her health. All her unprinted scripts were published by her husband.

AMERICAN WRITERS

Alberta Wilson Constant is well known for her popular and highly acclaimed novels, all of which describe the family lifestyle in the early twentieth century. She further went abroad to about neglect of women in politics. She was born in Texas, grew up in Tennessee, spent her school years in Oklahoma, and was graduated from Oklahoma City University. She was encouraged by several of her professors to write. Later, she took classes in professional writing at the University of Oklahoma. She is the mother of two grown children. Mrs. Constant lives with her husband in Independence, Missouri. She has contributed immensely to the success of female involvement in her region in America. She has also elevated the interest of youths in reading and writing. The following are the fascinating novels she has written.

Miss Charity Comes to Stay

Villie and the Wild Cat Veil

Paintbox on the Frontier: The life and Times of George

Caleb Binham

Those Miller Girls

The Motoring Millers

Does Anybody Care About Lou Emma Miller?

Each novel has its distinct form and style as presented by the author. Reading carefully each of her writing, one gets the idea of what she intends to convey. Her message in each novel, though lying basically on young ones and most importantly, pairing up youthful activities. It is very glaring that she has used the young ones to view her opinion of the main topic of her idea.

Young Lou Emma Miller was the only one that realized the need for Mrs. Biddle to become the mayor of Gloriosa. In essence, she had in mind to give her opinion that women needed to take part in politics.

All her novels relate the need for development and care for the growth of the young ones. Notwithstanding, she envisaged on love amidst families and cordial relationship in the community.

The Millers, The Biddles, Mr. Meadows and Miss Baker even the Colby's family, are all evidence of unconditional love.

Alberta Wilson Constant has won different awards on her novels and she is well known in the literary world of American Literature.

Joyce Carol Oates has often expressed an intense nostalgia for the time and place of her childhood and her working class upbringing is lovingly recalled in much of her fiction. Yet she had also admitted that the rural, rough and tumble surrounding of her early years involved a daily scramble of existence. Growing in the country side outside of Lockport, New York, she attended a one room school house in the elementary grades. As a child, she told stories instinctively by way of drawing and painting before learning how to write. After receiving the gift of a typewriter at age fourteen, she began consciously training herself, "writing novels after novels" throughout high school and college.

Success came early while attending Syracuse University on scholarship, she won the coveted mademoiselle fiction context. After graduating as valedictorian, she earned an M.A. in English at the University of Wisconsin where she met and married Richmond J. Smith after three months courtship in 1962. They settled in Detroit, a city whose erupting social tension suggested to Oates a microcosm of the violent American reality. Her finest early novel, then, along with steady stream of other novels and short stories, grew out of her Detroit experience. "Detroit my 'great' subject, she has written made me the person I am consequently, the writer I am-for better for worse."

Between 1968 and 1978, Oates taught at University of Windsor in Canada. She published books within two to three years. Though still in the thirties, she has become one of the most respected and honored writers, the United States of America.

She and her husband operate a small press and publish a literary magazine, "The Ontario Review". She taught in

Princeton University and shortly after her arrival, she began The Bellefleur. She wrote four novels of female experiences

– Solstice , Mary- A life and even a series of pseudonymous novels with the name Rosamond Smith.

AFRICAN WRITERS

AKACHI ADIMORA EZEIGBO

Akachi A dimora Ezeigbo is a native of Umuga in the Eastern region of Nigeria. She is a prolific writer and ardent promoter of the gender. Academically, she is a Professor of English Literature in the Department of English, University of Lagos, Nigeria. She has written many children story books and novels which have gained recognition in Nigeria and internationally. Knowing her personally has elevated my interest in writing, particularly when I read her trilogy for my thesis. She has encouraged many of her students to write about event familiar to them especially ones that would interest their readers. She particularly focuses her attention on women and individuality. Characters in her novels are portrayed in dignified way, which means she respects human capability in any form. Everybody is important in different perspectives. Almost all her writings are written with expertise, easy for any reader to comprehend. She has won several awards in Nigeria and abroad, including the noble prize winning of Spectrum Books. The following are the latest novels that fully brought her to limelight.

The Last of the Strong Ones

House of Symbols

Children of the Eagles

Echoes in the Mind

Each novel carries an aura of feminism and patriotism. Viewing Eaglewoman as the expected Okorigwe is the nostalgia of the female messiah who rid off the inferiority complex and male chauvinism, coming forth from the male counterpart of this era. She carried out vividly, strange and uncomely attitude of men against the weakness of women.

The House of Symbols introduces to one's mind the endurance to embrace in the face of trials.

Professor Akachi Adimora Ezeigbo, being the supervisor of this thesis, thanks and recognition are accorded for all the books and articles she has given me to be able to write effectively on this topic. The short poem is dedicated to her to show my appreciation.

More grease to your elbow

A woman of substance and virtue

One who, both gender adore to be

To you, honorable Akachi Adimora Ezeigbo.

JANE OLAMIDE OLUBUNMI

Jane Olamide Olubunmi is a prolific writer and a teacher of English Language and Literature. She was born in a little town, Ilesa in Nigeria. She had her elementary education and part of her secondary education in Lagos, the commercial capital of Nigeria. She volunteered to finish her secondary education in her home town, Ilesa, thus enabling her to be closer to her maternal grandmother, whose name she bears(Jane).

Jane was very close to granny and through conversations; she listened to her as she narrated the stories and myths of the Ijesa tribe.

She graduated from University of Ilorin, Kwara State, Nigeria and further on to have Master degree at University of Lagos, but finished up at National University, Republic of Benin. Prior to this time, she had started writing stories of her tribe and other fictions, which can be dated back to 1991. None of her books were published until 2004, which she must present for teaching at University of Abomey, Calavi, Republic of Benin. Black Maiden was read and reviewed by the first year students of the Department of English, University of Abomey, in 2004. Many of them wanted the continuation and conclusion of the book, already, the original book was in form of trilogy.

Her crave for writing further led her to write more which she submitted to Spectrum Books for publishing. She writes from the kindergarten to the university level, any literary works that can give awareness and understanding to the readers especially slow and naïve ones.

The following are the first books she wrote:

Black Maiden

Here at Last

The Eagle

Teens Crystal Memories

Each of her books carries distinct message for her readers. It is quite remarkable that she loves to narrate most of her stories. The first three books are in trilogy although, they were first written as one piece but because of the nature of her readers, she was advised to split them and publish them separately. Black Maiden leads on to Here at Last and in completion, The Eagle reveals the essence of the origin of the other two books.

Teens Crystal Memories is the reminiscence of her childhood. She narrates her autobiography in a distance for any child to fascinate and adult to embrace.

She is presently completing her doctorate degree under the supervision of the head of department, English, University of Abomey, Calavi, Republic of Benin. She will finish in the year 2005. She hopes to continue writing as she teaches in the institution.

CONCLUSION

The student's opinion on each text according to the topic "Comparative Study of Selected Female Writers as Seen in the Global Perspective.

I am obliged to select the authors in this thesis because of their uniqueness and devotion to writing as females. Uniqueness, in the sense that they have portrayed themselves capable of building what they feel has been controversial issue globally. Differently, women have been abused and are still suffering the neglect of their male counterpart. They have come in different ways, namely, marital as in Africa, loss of a partner or orphanage as in earlier time in Europe and politically as in America.

Jane Austen was highly indebted to all the characters used in her novels. She emphasized on each character, exposing not only the moral but physical comportment. It is hard to believe a woman at such era could be able to write effectively and create interest both in man and woman. Her novels were said to be widely read even when she was alive and men craved to have her as a wife. Although her opinion to remain unmarried even when she could have married the most dearest of all suitors remains a mystery except to excuse her as being fully engaged in her writings. Other things she engaged herself in were sewing and embroidery which most women took as profession at the time.

Fascinatingly, her novels create in the readers characters to emulate as in Mrs. Bennet who waited patiently for Mr. Bingley and Mr. Darcy to come and marry her two eldest daughters, as in Pride and Prejudice. Mrs. Norris in Mansfield Park whose character she described and thus put off any reader who might possess such as learning the end result and repercussion. She equally, related manners in men and women, embracing or rejecting them. William Collins' letter to the Bennets.

 Mr. Bennet's description gives the image of:

> "The person of whom I speak is a gentleman
>
> and a stranger."

Mary Lucas relates her opinion about Mr. Bingley:

> "His pride........ does not offend me so much as
>
> Pride often does, because this is an excuse for, it.
>
> One cannot wonder that so very a fine young man.
>
> with family, fortune, everything is his favor, should
>
> think highly of himself. If I may so express it, he

has a right to be proud."

The beginning of the novel relates the interactions of the Bennets, the Bingleys, Mr. Darcy and the Lucases. Other minor characters such as Mr. Hurst, who is Caroline's husband and Mr. Gardiner.

The relationships: Mr. Bingley and Jane

Mr. Darcy and Elizabeth

Mr. Collins and Elizabeth

Vickham and Lydia

Mr. Collins and Charlotte

The Georgianas

The suspense of the relations at the middle of the novel was to create recession whereby it would be finalized that love is not to be cheapened. Mrs. Bennet who match makes realizes her mistakes and keeps her breathe until the two glamorous young men come seeking for her first two daughters. The confrontation of the Lady of Borough, Lady Catherine depicts traditional convention of the time. Marrying her daughter off at birth to Mr. Darcy with consent of his mother shows how modesty rules not the order of the day.

The end justifies the means as the two sisters get married to the men of their choice after so much heart aches.

Nevertheless, happily married with Mr. and Mrs. Bennet consent and blessings, they resort to living with husbands at Derbyshire and somewhere not too far from each other.

CHARLOTTE BRONTE wrote extensively about orphanage and bereaved women. The Anglican Church at the time had orphanage homes which catered for orphans. Charlotte could have come across some children that prompted her to write about their biographies or narrate their autobiographies. It is clear that she felt compassion on all the major characters such as Jane Eyre, Lucy Snowe, Mrs. Bretton, a widow, Frances Evans Henry and possibly Professeur Emmanuel, all in different novels. Characters were not only her priority but settings of events.

Bretton was a location in an ancient town of England. It carried the name of the first settlers, Mr. and Mrs. Bretton, Lucy coming to stay with the Brettons was an exposure to characters different to what she earlier had with people of relation.

Villette was another fascinating town where Lucy stayed after leaving the Brettons. Villette was not only an ancient town but a place with fine weather and scenery. The novel Villette is enriched with characterizations and sceneries. There is the portray of love in genuine form, this excerpt gives us insight into Charlotte's version of innocent mind. Professeur Emanuel explains his mind to Lucy:

"Man cannot prophesy, love is an oracle

Fear sometimes imagine vain things."

Professeur Emmanuel declares to Lucy before traveling:

Lucy, take my love

One ay share my life, be my dearest,

first on earth.

Miss Percy is a novel that captures the imagination of the readers. The little girl, Percy whose father always come to the orphanage without caring how lonely she might be but to come and display his wealth. Miss Parcy, a pupil at

Turner's Seminary at Kessington exhibits her unhappiness and loneliness. Thus creating sorrow in the other children. Mrs. Turner could not have wished Percy to be whisked away by her father; she is one of the most influential.

Jane Eyre is the most popular of Charlotte's novels. She has been able to expose the incapability of a young orphan with the dejection and rejection which push her to the extremity of living in an orphanage home. The end of the story tells us that love prevails when all other things fail. Refusing St. John and coming hastily to marry Rochester depicts the nature of Charlotte as a person who admired the true love. St. John's letter, though does not include warm greetings of Jane's marriage to Rochester, it tells of his heavenly master:

"My master" he says has forewarned me.

Daily. He announces more distinctly surely

I come quickly! And hourly I move eagerly

Respond. Amen. Even so come Lord Jesus!

In other words, Charlotte is a dedicated Christian; this is evident in Jane Eyre and Villette.

Alberta Wilson Constant really impresses her readers by the dialogues which reveal emotions of her characters. It is amazing to read about a fifteen year old makes several discoveries about human nature while helping the local suffragettes elect the first woman mayor of Gloriosa, Kansas. Does Anybody Care About Lou Emma Miller? reveals the social and marital lives of the people of Gloriosa.

Professor Miller's relation with his wife and children, show the belief of the writer in securing good relationships. All along from the first novel, it has been painstaking occurrences. A good home like the Millers was hard to lose, the family stuck together despite all odds. Those Miller Girls is evident of an average American family.

"The happy family with all the wealth,

   no one could be compared with them.

   The merry go round as one unique.

   All it takes is love but what a pair!

Every one notices the Miller family

but none is yet to be." This is the critic observation.

The Motoring Millers reveals the prestige one has when someone has a motor car especially, one that is of a good make. The Motoring Millers having been able to purchase a good car like, the Great Smith. Professor Miller bought the car in order to convoy himself to school and to look different from the others. He quickly gets the respect and recognition he is looking for. Alberta Wilson Constant tries to expose people's respect for material acquisition such as respect for the Millers because of the Great Smith.

Does Anybody Care About Lou Emma Miller? further explains the plight of a young girl who feels unnoticed like her sister.

As if Maddy had been an only child,

as if I'd never been born. Or Barney.

Women's neglect in position is also obvious and Mrs. Biddle's plan is not welcome by the men. Also Miss Kate sees a positive change in Gloriosa if Mrs. Biddle becomes the mayor.

"It's going to be a hard scrap, Lou Emma,

Politics is a chancy business."

Constant tries to tell that women should be given the opportunity, rather than the benefit of the doubt.

At last a woman has an upper hand and becomes the mayoress of Gloriosa. The narration in the trilogy about women primarily concerns with recognition of women in politics and development. Thus Mrs. Biddle for the women and Lou Emma for the young females.

JOYCE CAROL OATES writes all over the aesthetical way. The dramatic trajectory of Oates career especially her amazing rise from economical straitened childhood to her current position as one of the world's most eminent authors , suggests a feminist, literary version of the mythic pursuit and achievement of American dream. Her teaching Bellefleur is the first in the series unofficially referred to as "The Gothic Quintet." The following are the thriller writings she has superciliously published.

> Bellefleur
>
> A Bloodsmoor Romance
>
> Mysteries of Winterthurn
>
> The Grosswicks Horror
>
> My Heart Laid Bare

America is a tale still being told by many voices and nowhere near its conclusion, Bellefleur is a novel about ambition for wealth and empire. It is more than a Gothic in its real sense. A Bloodsmoor Romance is full of sweet songs, hope and reality including the daughters of Zhin and America. The novel reveals plunging into the modern age as represented by the five daughters of Zhin. This is the classic tale our classics never dared reveal, the other side of little women as only Joyce Carol Oates can tell it. Bellefleur may be considered the mythic culmination of Joyce Carol Oates. As each of the Bellefleur follow his passions towards his ultimate fate, the novel moves to its surprising dramatic conclusion. A remarkable, ongoing portrait of American life.

Mysteries of Winterthurn evokes in the reader fear and agony of the characters who are abused. Xavier represents the traditional hero while Perdita represents innocence and the murdered girls are victims of cruelty.

> After the struggle to solve the mystery of the
>
> Blood stained Bridal Gown. He is able to solve
>
> Triple murder cases…………………

In the three novels, it is important to know that all the characters in essence are displayed in form or create in our minds what the author wants to convey. For example, Germaine in Bellefleur, the three daughters of Zhin and Xavier in Mysteries of Winterthurn are pure representative of the emergence of American modernity.

The works of Joyce Carol Oates mark the emergence of America civilization. She is seen to have suffered the pain to put every of her idea down on paper. All the same in order to make herself well understood, she opted out to use the thriller stylish method. The Gothic method she has used helps to create in our minds the atrocities of the people of a country amidst growth. Bellefleur has produced this vividly:

> "........wealthy and notorious clan in the region not
>
> unlike the Aderondarics- in an enormous mansion
>
> in the shores of mythical Lake Noir, a prolific and
>
> eccentric group- they include millionaires, a mass
>
> murderer, a spiritual seeker who climbs into the
>
> mountains looking for God.

It is important to know the meaning of Gothic stylish writing. Elements of the Gothic novels took shape mostly in England from 1790-1830 and falls within the category of Romantic Literature. It acts however, as a reaction against the rigidity and formality of other forms of Romantic Literature. The hero becomes a sort of archetype as we find that there is a pattern to their characterization. There is always the protagonist, usually isolated either voluntarily. Then there is the villain who is the epitome of evil either by his (usually a man) own fall from grass or by some implicit malevolence.

The wanderer found in many Gothic Tales is the epitome of isolation as he wanders the earth perpetual exile, usually a form of divine punishment. The plot itself mirrors the ruined world in its dealings with a protagonist's fall from grace as she succumbs to temptation from a villain. In the end the protagonist must be saved through a reunion with a loved one.

Gothic could mean a particular style of art, such as, novels, paintings or architecture. It could mean music and its focus. It could mean "medieval or uncouth'"

Original meaning, relating the Gothic, their civilization or their language, ("gothic"). The New Gothic tends to focus upon interior state of mind, there are no cartoon monster in The New Gothic.

Oates recognizes, however, a distinct on the popular sense of horror as opposed to horror in the literary sense.

> "........the mystery of the blood stained
>
> Bridal Gown."

AKACHI ADIMORA EZEIGBO is not a narrow minded writer because of how she has portrayed her female characters differently to suit her objectives. Her characterization of women are properly adjusted members of the community with parallel line of authority in traditional governance, they assert themselves and respected in their own domain. She undertakes an excursion into the socio-cultural-political nature of the Igbo society. She alters the patrilineal style that dominated in the early Nigerian fiction as the same engagement by introducing a strong female perception.

The time and space covered by the novel is the colonial era in Nigeria, with emphasis on the Umuga community in the novelist native Anambra State. The novelty of the white man's religion, with its paradox an d more especially his system of administration, the warrant chiefs, made up the local rulers which leads itself to misadministration. They do not go down well with influential woman groups in the society, who see the need to assent traditional bulwark for redemption purpose.

She evokes brave African women who believe among others, bearding the lion in his den. Three significant groups which hold strong society. Umuda, Oluada and the Obuofo, Umuda are mothers who hold strong opinion, Oluada, they are selected group, four women representing women in the local council. Obuofo is the inner council and together, they deliberate on significant happenings and events, often useful advice executing actions when necessary.

Ejimnaka sighed with satisfaction and continued, "Obuofo will meet tomorrow to discuss the stubbornness and uncooperative attitude of Okwara, the warrant chief. This is why we are meeting this morning to agree on a common point."

The crisis in the novel is generated by the protest on the letter written by women to Kosiri on the failure of his warrant chief, Okwara, to the cause of the people. The Kosiri interprets their action as rebellious and plan a war. It claims casualty on both sides leading to eventual defeat of the Umuga warriors with superior fire power. Yet the war brings out the best in women amazons in terms of intellectual contributions.

The novel rings with substances from its intertextual dimensions, its feminism and maternal bounding for female empowerment.

The second novel, House of Symbols is the reincarnation of two fortified figures. Okwara and Ejimnaka whose offspring eventually becomes one identity by marriage. Josiah Okwara cannot avoid the admiration of the young woman from the lineage of such powerful ardent controller of women of early Umuga.

It is the ancestral cause of Okwara family that debars his wife from getting pregnant. The House of Symbols signifies the two ancestral origins and claims- Okwara and Ejimnaka. Josiah represents his ancestor while his wife represents her ancestor. The two notable figures are making up their differences in their successors. The unity and peace which could not hold between the two are evidently established through the marriage of these young couple.

Mr. and Mrs.Okwara, are exemplary figures in the society who feel for the poor and the needy. Mrs. Okwara is more enthusiastic about doing one thing or the other for the poor, which is often to the fascination of her husband. Reincarnation of a dead one as prophesied by the prophetess depicts belief of a new religion which has replaced the old one.

The death of Josiah Okwara has created a great vacuum in the life of Mrs. Okwara. The writer has been brought out attributes for readers to fancy and emulate.

The third novel, Children of the Eagle is most importantly, of social reconstruction. The greatest achievement of the novel lies in the writers ability to move beyond mere exposition of the social crimes against women to powerfully demonstrate though the lives of the main characters the ways out of such degradation. The five enviable daughters of Eaglewoman do not just sit down and bemoan the ignoble state of women in Umuga; rather they map and carry out strategies that change the state of affairs. For example, they do not merely bemoan the insult of Umeeku's sons nor are they discouraged by the fact that the highest decision-making body in the land will not deal fairly with them.

For writer, the feminist struggle is not only external but also internal, working hard with a firm determination to succeed. The feminism of the writer is basically African and hence liberal. It can therefore be referred to as "womanism" in order to differentiate it from the separatist nature of radical Western feminism.

Jane Olamide Olubunmi's Black Maiden is a histo-romantic story. It conveys to the readers the greatness of a kingdom through narration and the love affairs of a maiden with two men. The story is a mixture of narration and poetic words.

Superbly written, though with simple reflections of figures of speech.

> Thou art like the lilies of the valley.

> Thou art fair like the lilies of the valley.

> Thou art comely my queen…………..

The speech made by king Adewale to the queen , Olori Oriade is to show his admiration of his beauty. Hatred, love, conspiracy, dejection and war are evident in the story. Hatred is noticed at the beginning of the story when Aderopo, the eldest son of a king do not allow his younger brother to claim the throne as instructed by his father before his death. Adewale leaves his father's land and goes somewhere to go and establish a kingdom. He goes away to avoid the wrath of his brother. Love is not farfetched for Duduyemi, first with the king of Ilasa. King Adewale cannot reject the gift sent from king of Ajele. He changes her name to Duduyemi to show his affection and how much he admires her. Later on in the story, there appears Aladeju, who takes permission from Duduyemi's father, the king of

Ajele to come in search of her. This character presents himself as the fiancé of Duduyemi. He arrives at Ilasa and at the riverside; they exchange songs which show love displayed by two young people.

> My beloved is mine, I am his.
>
> His banner over me is love.

Conspiracy is seen in the attitude of Olori Oriade and Fabunmi against Duduyemi.

> He, he, he, laughed Olori Oriade.
>
> Why are you laughing, asked Fabunmi.
>
> I saw the king and Duduyemi……..replied Olori
>
> Oriade.

The elders cannot hide their feeling about the oracle's proclamation, though king Adewale disregards the message.

War is seen as a regular act in the story which leads to the acquisition of slaves and the expansion of the kingdom. The trial of Duduyemi and her condemnation by the king is declaring judgment without being sentimental.

Here at Last further tells us about Duduyemi and Aladeju and what becomes of them. Determination of Aladeju to elope with Duduyemi is obvious in the early part of the story:

Let us go quietly away before dawn.

The yard will be quiet and people asleep.

They escape and Duduyemi gives birth to a child during their journey back. The king does not take it lightly, he sends warriors to destroy Ajele and they return to a ruined kingdom. Aladeju plans to rebuild it, which he does and warns his son to be peaceful with other kingdoms around him during his tenure.

The Eagle reveals the successors of the people earlier on mentioned in the two books. Here, an orator opens up the story by telling a story to his grandchildren. There are series of activities such as the occupations of the people, age group, marriage, monarchy, wars and trafficking of slaves. The orator, though, he is the narrator, appears at the end of the story to answer the questions his grandchildren ask concerning the white men that engage in slave trafficking.

BIBLIOGRAPHY

ARTICLES

Article on the Jane Eyre by Richard Alleva

Articles on Children of the Eagle by Guardian Newspaper Nigeria.

Article on Black Maiden National Newspaper Republic of Benin.

BOOKS

Encyclopidea Britanica Volume L, A, B, O, C.

Chronicle in Literature by Copper.

READING TEXTS

Jane Austen:

Pride and Prejudice

Sense and Sensibility

Mansfield Park

Persuasion

Emma

Charlotte Bronte:

Jane Eyre

The Professor

Villette

Miss Percy

Alberta Wilson Constant:

Those Miller Girls

The Motoring Millers

Does Anybody Care About Lou Emma Miller?

Joyce Carol Oates:

Bellefleur

Bloodsmoor Romance

Mysteries of Winterthurn

Akachi Adimora Ezeigbo:

The Last of the Strong Ones

Children of the Eagle

House of Symbols

Jane Olamide Olubunmi:

Black Maiden

Here at Last

The Eagle